Easy Bake Oven
Cookbook

Develop Child's Hands-On Skills and Interest In
Cooking with Easy-To-Follow Recipes

Shanna Lerma

Table of Contents

Introduction

Let's begin with the endless possibilities of culinary experience tailored for young chefs and aspiring bakers, where the magic of miniature ovens meets the happiness of creating delectable treats. The Easy Bake Oven has been a beloved kitchen companion for generations, inspiring countless children to discover the joys of baking, experimenting, and sharing their delectable creations. Now, we invite you to start on a delicious journey as we present "The Easy Bake Oven Recipe Book" – a delightful compilation of recipes that will ignite your culinary imagination.

What Is Easy Bake Oven?

History

Before we talk about the recipes, let's take a moment to understand the basics of the Easy Bake Oven for those who might be encountering it for the first time. The Easy Bake Oven is a compact, electric oven designed for young bakers. It operates at a low temperature, making it safe and easy for children to use. Its compact size is perfect for small hands, and it comes with a variety of baking utensils and accessories that make the baking process not only manageable but also fun.

The Easy-Bake Oven made its debut in 1963, introduced by the Kenner Products Company, an American toy company. It was originally conceived as a children's toy that could replicate the experience of baking in a real oven but in a safe and

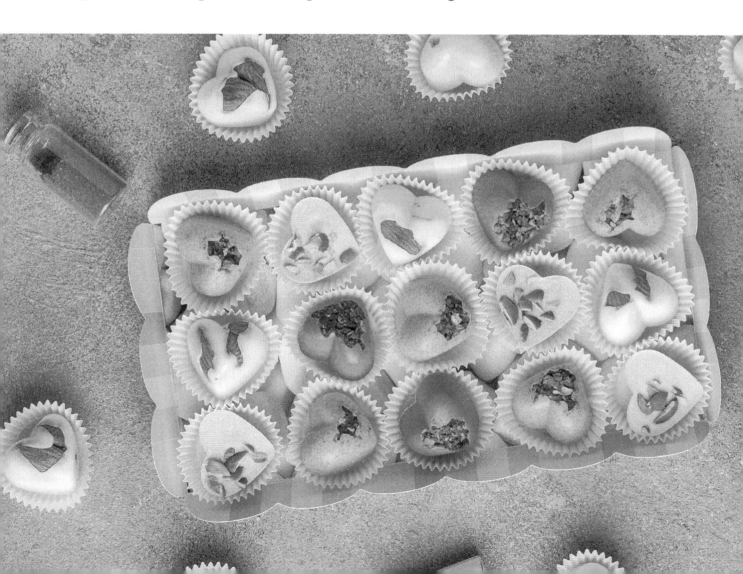

scaled-down manner. The design of the Easy-Bake Oven was inspired by the idea of allowing children, particularly young girls, to explore the happiness of baking without the risks associated with using a traditional oven. The initial Easy-Bake Oven model was a turquoise and white oven that came with a carrying handle and a heating element powered by a regular incandescent light bulb. It included miniature cake mixes and baking pans, and the first version was sold for around $15.95. This early version became an instant hit and laid the foundation for the decades of success that would follow. The Easy-Bake Oven became culturally significant during this era, reflecting the societal expectations and gender roles of the time. It was primarily marketed towards girls, reinforcing traditional stereotypes of women as homemakers. Despite these limitations, the toy provided an opportunity for young girls to develop basic culinary skills and creativity.

During the 1980s and 1990s, the Easy-Bake Oven underwent several changes and updates to keep up with the changing times and evolving tastes of its young users.

One of the significant innovations during this period was the introduction of a variety of oven designs and colors to appeal to a broader audience. Additionally, the light bulb heating element was replaced with a safer heating element that used a heating element and no longer relied on incandescent bulbs. This improved safety and efficiency while preserving the essence of the toy. Kenner expanded the Easy-Bake product line to include a wider range of food options, such as pizzas, pretzels, brownies, and more. This expansion allowed children to experiment with different types of recipes and flavors, encouraging creativity in the kitchen. The Easy-Bake Oven continued to adapt and evolve in response to changing consumer preferences and safety standards. In the early 2000s, it faced a significant redesign in response to safety concerns about the heating elements. In 2007,

there were reports of children getting their hands caught in the oven's opening, which led to a recall. Subsequently, the oven underwent a substantial redesign with enhanced safety features. The modern Easy-Bake Oven features a sleeker design with a compartment for mixing and a separate heating chamber. It uses an enclosed, electric heating element, eliminating the need for light bulbs. These design changes addressed safety concerns and ensured the oven's continued popularity. In recent years, Hasbro, the company that acquired Kenner Products, has been more inclusive in its marketing, emphasizing that the Easy-Bake Oven is for children of all genders. This shift reflects changing societal attitudes and the recognition that culinary skills should be accessible to all.

The Easy-Bake Oven holds a unique place in the history of children's toys. It has not only introduced generations of children to the joys of baking but has also contributed to the development of basic culinary skills and creativity. The enduring popularity of the Easy-Bake Oven highlights its timeless appeal, and it continues to be cherished by children and collectors alike. Easy-Bake Oven has a rich and evolving history that reflects not only changes in toy design and technology but also shifts in societal norms and expectations.

From its humble beginnings in the 1960s to its modern iterations, it has left an indelible mark on the world of toys and culinary education for children.

A World of Possibilities in a Tiny Oven

The Easy Bake Oven has long been a cherished part of many childhoods. For over half a century, it has brought smiles, laughter, and a sense of accomplishment to countless young bakers. This remarkable miniature oven may be small in size, but it offers limitless possibilities when it comes to creating scrumptious goodies. Whether you're whipping up a classic chocolate chip cookie or crafting a mini gourmet meal, the Easy Bake Oven is your portal to the world of baking.

Baking as a Creative Experience

Baking is a creative experience that transcends the simple act of combining ingredients to produce a finished product. It is an art form that allows individuals to express themselves, experiment with flavors and textures, and craft something unique with their own hands. This creativity is evident in every step of the baking process, from the selection of ingredients to the final presentation of the baked goods. At the heart of baking's creative allure is the selection of ingredients. Each ingredient contributes not only to the taste but also to the overall texture and appearance of the final product. Bakers carefully choose ingredients, considering the quality of the flour, the sweetness of the sugar, the richness of the butter, and the freshness of the eggs. These choices influence the character of the baked goods and provide a canvas upon which the baker can paint their culinary masterpiece. Creativity in baking truly flourishes during the recipe development and adaptation process. Bakers often take inspiration from traditional recipes but then add their

unique twist. This could involve incorporating unexpected ingredients, such as herbs in a bread recipe or exotic spices in a cookie. It's a playful exploration of flavors that can lead to exciting discoveries and signature creations. The artistry extends to the presentation of baked goods. The aesthetic appeal of a beautifully decorated cake or intricately shaped bread is a testament to the baker's creativity. Decorating with frosting, glazes, or intricate designs allows for personal expression and adds an extra layer of visual delight to the finished product. Every sprinkle, drizzle, or meticulously placed berry is an opportunity to showcase creativity.

A Nostalgic Nod to the Past

For those who grew up with the Easy Bake Oven, this recipe book is a trip back in time, a nostalgic reminder of the hours spent concocting mini masterpieces in the warm glow of a tiny oven light. The joy of sharing these moments with friends and family, the sense of accomplishment when a creation turned out just right, and the occasional mishap that became a cherished memory – it's all part of the Easy Bake Oven experience.

How the Easy Bake Oven Works?

The Easy Bake Oven works by heating a small incandescent light bulb, which in turn radiates heat into the baking chamber. The oven comes with baking pans, trays, and utensils designed to fit its petite dimensions. The low heat ensures that young bakers can safely prepare their treats without the risk of burns or accidents, making it an excellent introduction to the world of baking.

Before First Use

Safety First: As with any kitchen activity, safety is of paramount importance. Before using the Easy Bake Oven, always ensure that adult supervision is available, especially for younger children. Make sure to follow all safety guidelines provided in the oven's instruction manual, and teach children the importance of kitchen safety practices, such as proper handling of hot pans and utensils.

Benefits of Using It

The Art of Baking

Baking is not just about following a recipe; it's about the happiness of creating something delicious from scratch. It's about experimenting with flavors, textures, and ingredients to produce an art that tantalizes the taste buds and warms the heart. In this recipe book, we'll guide you through the fundamentals of baking, helping you master the art of measuring, mixing, and baking.

The Ingredients

Every great recipe begins with high-quality ingredients. From flour and sugar to eggs and butter, we'll explore the role each ingredient plays in your baked creations. We'll also discuss ingredient substitutions, so you can adapt recipes to suit dietary restrictions or personal preferences.

The Techniques

Baking is as much about technique as it is about ingredients. We'll walk you through

essential baking techniques, such as creaming, folding, and kneading. You'll learn how to achieve the perfect consistency for your batters and dough, ensuring that your treats turn out just right every time.

The Tools

In addition to the Easy Bake Oven itself, you'll need some basic tools and utensils to make the baking process smooth and enjoyable. We'll introduce you to these essential tools and provide tips on how to use them effectively. From pan pusher and spatula to mixing bowls, you'll soon become familiar with the baker's toolkit.

The Recipes

Now, the heart of "The Easy Bake Oven Recipe Book" – the recipes themselves. Our collection spans a wide range of delectable treats, from classic cookies and brownies to savory mini pizzas and quiches. Whether you're in the mood for a sweet indulgence or a savory delight, there's a recipe here to satisfy your craving.

Sweet Treats

Indulge your sweet tooth with a variety of cookie, cake, and pastry recipes. Discover the joy of making miniature cupcakes, delightful fruit tarts, and gooey chocolate chip cookies that will have everyone begging for more. Our easy-to-follow instructions will ensure your sweet creations turn out perfectly every time.

Special Occasions

Baking is a wonderful way to celebrate special occasions, and we've included recipes that are perfect for birthdays, holidays, and other memorable moments. From miniature birthday cakes to festive holiday cookies, these recipes will help you add a personal touch to your celebrations.

Savory Delights

For those who prefer savory over sweet, we've got you covered. Dive into a world of savory mini pizzas, cheesy quesadillas, and flavorful quiches that make for a perfect snack or light meal. You'll learn how to create these savory bites with the same enthusiasm and skill as your sweet treats.

Baking Beyond Boundaries

While the Easy Bake Oven is designed with young bakers in mind, it's not just for kids. Baking transcends age, and this recipe book is suitable for anyone who wants to explore the world of miniature baking. It's an opportunity for parents, guardians, and caregivers to bond with their children in the kitchen, creating lasting memories and passing down the joy of baking through generations.

"The Easy Bake Oven Recipe Book" is more than just a collection of recipes; it's an invitation to start a culinary experience filled with creativity, joy, and deliciousness. Whether you're a seasoned Easy Bake Oven veteran or a newcomer eager to explore the world of miniature baking, this book is your guide to unlocking the magic of the tiny oven.

So, gather your ingredients, preheat your Easy Bake Oven, and let's get started on a journey of delectable discovery. With each recipe you create, you'll not only fill your kitchen with wonderful aromas but also your heart with the satisfaction of creating something truly special.

Chapter 1 Cake and Brownie Recipes

Cinnamon Blueberry Shortcake

Prep Time: 10 minutes | Cook Time: 10 minutes | Serves: 4

¼ cup biscuit mix
5 teaspoons milk
Blueberries
1 tablespoon sugar
⅛ teaspoon cinnamon
Cool whip

1. Plug in your Easy-Bake Ultimate Oven and preheat for 15 minutes. 2. With a fork, mix biscuit mix and milk. Make two equal parts. Roll each one out on a floured surface until it fits the baking pan. Put each one in the oiled baking pan. 3. Lay the baking pan into the Easy-Bake Ultimate Oven's baking slot. 4. With the help of a pan pusher, push the baking pan into the baking chamber. 5. Adjust the cooking time to 10 minutes and bake. 6. After the cooking time ends, push the baking pan into the cooling chamber with the help of a pan pusher. Allow it to cool for 10 minutes. 7. When cooling is done, with the help of a spatula, remove the baking pan from the oven. 8. In a different bowl, mix sugar, cinnamon, and blueberries. 9. Put in a bowl, then add blueberries and cool whip on top.

White Chocolate Cake

Prep Time: 10 minutes | Cook Time: 12–15 minutes | Serves: 2

1 package yellow cake mix
3 tablespoons white chocolate pudding mix
2 tablespoons plus 1 teaspoon milk

1. Mix the cake mix, pudding mix, and milk in a bowl. Stir until the batter is smooth. 2. Pour the batter into the Easy-Bake Oven baking pan. You'll need to bake in batches. 3. Bake each batch in the Easy-Bake Oven for 12–15 minutes or until the sides of the cake separate from the pan. 4. Remove and allow to cool completely.

Ginger Pineapple Cake

Prep Time: 8 minutes | Cook Time: 9 minutes | Serves: 2

2 yellow cake mixes
⅛ teaspoon ground cinnamon
2 pinches ground nutmeg
2 pinches ground ginger
1 tablespoon carrots; shredded
2 teaspoons pineapple; drained, crushed
1 teaspoon egg, beaten
2½ teaspoons water
Cream cheese frosting

1. Plug in your Easy-Bake Ultimate Oven and preheat for 15 minutes. 2. Greasing and flour baking pan for Easy-Bake Oven. 3. Mix all the ingredients except the frosting until well blended. 4. Pour half of the mixture into the baking pan. 5. Lay the baking pan into the Easy-Bake Ultimate Oven's baking slot. 6. With the help of a pan pusher, push the baking pan into the baking chamber. 7. Adjust the cooking time to 9 minutes and bake. 8. After the cooking time ends, push the baking pan into the cooling chamber with the help of a pan pusher. Allow it to cool for 5 minutes. 9. When cooling is done, with the help of a spatula, remove the baking pan from the oven. 10. Plate the cake and spread cream cheese frosting over with the help of a spatula. Serve and enjoy.

Vanilla Cocoa Brownie

Prep Time: 10 minutes | Cook Time: 12 minutes | Serves: 12

1 tablespoon water
2 tablespoons flour
Anti-sticking baking spray
1 tablespoon olive oil
2 tablespoons sugar
½ teaspoon vanilla
1 tablespoon cocoa powder

1. Plug in the easy bake oven, preheating it for 15 minutes. 2. Spritz baking spray on the baking pan, followed by dusting with flour. 3. In a bowl, merge cocoa powder with all other ingredients and whisk to incorporate. 4. Lay batter onto the baking pan. 5. Bake in the preheated oven for 12 minutes. 5. After cooking time is finished, give it about five minutes to cool down. 6. Carefully turn the brownies onto a platter to serve and enjoy.

Easy Devil's Food Cake

Prep Time: 15 minutes | Cook Time: 15 minutes | Serves: 8

1 package yellow cake mix
2 tablespoons milk
3 tablespoons pudding mix, Devil's food
Anti-sticking baking spray

1. Plug in the easy bake oven, preheating it for 15 minutes. 2. Spray the Easy-Bake Oven baking pan with baking spray and then dust lightly with flour. 3. Put all the ingredients into medium-sized bowl and whisk to incorporate. 4. Drizzle the mixture into the prepared pan. 5. Lay out the mixture onto the baking pan. 6. Bake in the preheated oven for 15 minutes. 7. After cooking time is finished, with pan pusher, shove the baking pan into the "Cooling Chamber". 8. Give it about five minutes to cool down. 9. Turn the cake carefully onto a dish so it can cool completely before serving.

Lemon Delight Trifle

Prep Time: 10 minutes | Cook Time: 15 minutes | Serves: 3

6 tablespoons yellow cake mix
2 tablespoons milk
1 small box lemon instant pudding mix
1½ cups cold milk
1 small cool whip; softened

1. Plug in your Easy-Bake Ultimate Oven and preheat for 15 minutes. 2. Add 2 tablespoons of milk to the yellow cake mix and mix it well. 3. Put them in round cake pan from the Easy-Bake Oven. 4. Bake in the preheated oven for 15 minutes and bake. 5. After the cooking time ends, push the baking pan into the cooling chamber with the help of a pan pusher. Allow it to cool for 5 minutes. 6. When cooling is done, with the help of spatula, remove the baking pan from the oven. 7. Cut into pieces that are easy to eat. 8. Add the pudding mix to the rest of the milk. 9. Add cool whip and mix it in. 10. Put pieces of one cake on the bottom of a dessert dish or glass bowl. 11. Put some pudding mix on top. 12. Do it again for more layers. 13. Put in the fridge until ready to serve.

Pineapple Cake

Prep Time: 10 minutes | Cook Time: 20 minutes | Serves: 3

1 pack yellow cake mix
6 teaspoons pineapple juice
2 tablespoon crushed pineapple
1 tablespoon butter
2 teaspoon brown sugar

1. Plug in your Easy-Bake Ultimate Oven and preheat for 15 minutes. 2. Put the cake mix and pineapple juice together and mix them. 3. Put 1 tablespoon of butter in the baking pan and melt it. 4. Put a little brown sugar on the bottom of the pan. 5. Put one tablespoon of crushed pineapple on top of the brown sugar. 6. Use a spoon to lightly mash the food. Add cake batter on top of the pineapples. 7. Bake in the preheated oven for 20 minutes. 8. After the cooking time ends, push the baking pan into the cooling chamber with the help of a pan pusher. Allow it to cool for 5 minutes. 9. When cooling is done, with the help of spatula, remove the baking pan from the oven. 10. Place the cake on a plate and stand the pineapple on top of it.

Pink Velvet Cake

Prep Time: 10 minutes | Cook Time: 15 minutes | Serves: 3

5 tablespoons flour
¼ teaspoon baking powder
⅛ teaspoon salt
5 teaspoons red sugar crystals
¼ teaspoon vanilla
4 teaspoons vegetable oil
8 teaspoons milk
1 cup white frosting

1. Plug in your Easy-Bake Ultimate Oven and preheat for 15 minutes. 2. Mix everything together except the frosting until the batter is smooth and pink. 3. Put 3 tablespoons of batter into an Easy-Bake Oven cake pan that has been greased. 4. Bake in the preheated oven for 15 minutes. 5. After the cooking time ends, push the baking pan into the cooling chamber with the help of a pan pusher. Allow it to cool for 5 minutes. 6. When cooling is done, with the help of spatula, remove the baking pan from the oven. 7. Do the same for second layer again. 8. Place the cake on the plate and pour frosting than add second layer on top. Serve and enjoy.

Pink Barbie Cake

Prep Time: 10 minutes | Cook Time: 15 minutes | Serves: 4

5 tablespoons flour
¼ teaspoon baking powder
⅛ teaspoon salt
5 teaspoons red home-made colored sugar
¼ teaspoon vanilla
4 teaspoons vegetable oil
8 teaspoons milk
Barbie's sparkling frosting

1. Plug in your Easy-Bake Ultimate Oven and preheat for 15 minutes. 2. Cake flour, baking powder, salt, red sugar, vanilla, oil, and milk should all be mixed together until the batter is smooth and pink. 3. Put three tablespoons of batter into the baking pan that has been oiled and dusted. 4. Lay out the baking pan into the Easy-Bake Ultimate Oven's baking slot. 5. With the help of a pan pusher, push the baking pan into the baking chamber. 6. Adjust the cooking time to 15 minutes and bake. 7. After the cooking time ends, push the baking pan into the cooling chamber with the help of a pan pusher. Allow it to cool for 5 minutes. 8. When cooling is done, with the help of spatula, remove the baking pan from the oven. 9. Put Barbie's Sparkling Frosting on top. It makes two layers.

Homemade Coconut Pudding Cake

Prep Time: 10 minutes | Cook Time: 15 minutes | Serves: 4

1 package yellow cake mix
2 tablespoons milk
3 tablespoons coconut cream pudding mix
1 teaspoon shredded coconut

1. Plug in your Easy-Bake Ultimate Oven and preheat for 15 minutes. 2. The Easy-Bake Oven baking pan should be greased and floured. 3. Put everything but the coconut into a small bowl and stir them together until the mixture is smooth. 4. Put the batter into the prepared pan, and then sprinkle coconut on top. 5. Bake in the preheated oven for 12-15 minutes.

Flavorful Carrot Pineapple Cake

Prep Time: 10 minutes | Cook Time: 9 minutes | Serves: 6

2 packages yellow cake mix
⅛ teaspoon ground cinnamon
2 pinches ground nutmeg
2 pinches ground ginger
1 tablespoon grated carrots
2 teaspoons canned crushed pineapple
1 teaspoon beaten egg
2½ teaspoons water
Cream cheese frosting

1. Plug in your Easy-Bake Ultimate Oven and preheat for 15 minutes. 2. Oil and flour the Easy Bake baking pan. 3. Mix everything together and stir it around until it's well blended. Put the mix into the pan. 4. Bake in the preheated oven for 9 minutes. 5. After the cooking time ends, push the baking pan into the cooling chamber with the help of a pan pusher. Allow it to cool for 5 minutes. 6. When cooling is done, with the help of spatula, remove the baking pan from the oven. 7. Spread cream cheese frosting around the cake and cut in half. Make them two layers and serve.

Peanut Butter Cake

Prep Time: 10 minutes | Cook Time: 12-15 minutes | Serves: 4

6 tablespoons flour
4 teaspoons sugar
¼ teaspoon baking powder
Dash salt
6 teaspoons milk
2 teaspoons peanut butter frosting of your choice
⅛ vanilla extract

1. Plug in your Easy-Bake Ultimate Oven and preheat for 15 minutes. 2. Add the salt, baking powder, flour, and sugar to a bowl. 3. Mix the peanut butter, milk, and vanilla extract together until the mixture is smooth. 4. Put the batter into an Easy Bake Oven cake pan that has been greased and dusted. 5. Bake in the preheated oven for 12-15 minutes.

Vanilla Cocoa Cake

Prep Time: 10 minutes | Cook Time: 15 minutes | Serves: 1

Anti-sticking baking spray
4 teaspoons all-purpose flour
2 teaspoons cocoa powder
1 tablespoon sugar
⅛ teaspoon baking powder
1 pinch of salt
⅛ teaspoon vanilla extract
4 teaspoons water
2 teaspoons vegetable oil

1. Preheat your Easy-Bake Ultimate Oven for 15 minutes. 2. Spray the Easy-Bake Oven baking pan with baking spray. 3. Put flour and remnant ingredients into a small-sized bowl and blend to form a smooth mixture. 4. Put the mixture into the prepared baking pan. 5. Lay out the baking pan into the "Baking Slot" of Easy-Bake Ultimate Oven. 6. With a pan pusher, push the baking pan into the "Baking Chamber". 7. Set the cooking time for 13-15 minutes. 8. After cooking time is finished, with a pan pusher, push the baking pan into the "Cooling Chamber". 9. Let it cool for around 5 minutes. 10. Turn off the oven and with a spatula, take off the baking pan from the oven. 11. Transfer the baking pan to a counter to cool for around 10 minutes. Enjoy!

Tasty Strawberry Cake

Prep Time: 10 minutes | Cook Time: 10 minutes | Serves: 2

Anti-sticking baking spray
6 teaspoons all-purpose flour
4 teaspoons sugar
1 teaspoon strawberry drink mix
¼ teaspoon baking soda
1 pinch of salt
¾ teaspoon shortening
6 teaspoons milk

1. Preheat your Easy-Bake Ultimate Oven for 15 minutes. 2. Spray the Easy-Bake Oven baking pan with baking spray. 3. Put flour and remnant ingredients except the shortening and the milk into a bowl and blend to incorporate thoroughly. 4. Put in shortening and blend to incorporate thoroughly. 5. Slowly put in milk and blend to form a smooth and creamy mixture. 6. Transfer the mixture into the prepared baking pan. 7. Bake in the preheated oven for 10 minutes. 8. Carefully take off the cake from the baking pan and shift onto a plate to cool thoroughly before enjoying.

Fluffy Banana Cream Pudding Cake

Prep Time: 10 minutes | Cook Time: 30 minutes | Serves: 2

Anti-sticking baking spray
6 tablespoons all-purpose flour
4 teaspoons sugar
¼ teaspoon baking powder
1 pinch of salt
6 teaspoons milk
2 teaspoons shortening
3 tablespoons banana cream pudding mix

1. Preheat your Easy-Bake Ultimate Oven for 15 minutes. 2. Spray the Easy-Bake Oven baking pan with baking spray and then dust with a little flour. 3. Put the flour, sugar, baking powder and salt into a bowl and blend to incorporate. 4. Put milk and shortening and blend to form a smooth mixture. 5. Put in pudding mix and blend to incorporate. 6. Transfer the mixture into the prepared baking pan. 7. Bake in the preheated oven for 12-15 minutes. 8. After cooking time is finished, with a pan pusher, push the "Baking Pan" into the "Cooling Chamber". Let it cool for around 5 minutes. 9. Carefully take off the cake from the baking pan and shift onto a plate to cool thoroughly before enjoying.

Coconut Chocolate Fudge Cake

Prep Time: 10 minutes | Cook Time: 30 minutes | Serves: 2

Anti-sticking baking spray
6 tablespoons flour
4 teaspoons sugar
3 tablespoons chocolate fudge pudding mix
1 teaspoon coconut, shredded
¼ teaspoon baking powder
1 pinch of salt
6 teaspoons milk
2 teaspoons shortening
¼ teaspoon vanilla extract

1. Preheat your Easy-Bake Ultimate Oven for 15 minutes. 2. Spray the Easy-Bake Oven baking pan with baking spray. 3. Put flour and remnant ingredients into a bowl and blend to form a smooth mixture. 4. Place the mixture into the prepared baking pan. 5. Bake in the preheated oven for 12-15 minutes. 6. After cooking time is finished, with a pan pusher, push the "Baking Pan" into the "Cooling Chamber". Let it cool for around 5 minutes. 7. Carefully take off the cake from the baking pan and shift onto a plate to cool thoroughly.

Colorburst Cake

Prep Time: 10 minutes | Cook Time: 15 minutes | Serves: 2

½ cup white or yellow cake mix
2 tablespoons water
¼ teaspoon vanilla extract
1 tablespoon rainbow sprinkles

1. Combine the white or yellow cake mix, water, and vanilla extract. Stir until the batter is smooth and free of lumps. 2. Preheat the easy-bake oven for about 15 minutes. 3. Gently fold the rainbow sprinkles into the cake batter. This will give your cake a colorful appearance. On the other hand, grease the Oven cake pan with non-stick cooking spray to prevent the cake from sticking. 4. Spread the mixture in the pan. 5. Carefully place the cake pan into the preheated Oven. Bake for approximately 12-15 minutes or until the cake has risen and a toothpick or cake tester inserted into the center comes out clean. Once the cake is done baking, place it for cooling.

Vanilla Cake

Prep Time: 10 minutes | Cook Time: 15 minutes | Serves: 2

½ cup vanilla cake mix
2 tablespoons water
Non-stick cooking spray
Vanilla frosting and sprinkles for decoration

1. Preheat the easy bake oven for 15 minutes. 2. In a mixing bowl, combine the vanilla cake mix and water. Stir the mixture until a smooth batter forms. Ensure there are no lumps. 3. Pour the prepared cake batter into the greased cake pan, spreading it evenly to ensure uniform baking. 4. Carefully place the cake pan into the preheated Easy Bake Oven. Bake the cake for approximately 12-15 minutes. Keep an eye on it to prevent overcooking. The cake is done when a toothpick or cake tester inserted into the center comes out clean. 5. Once done, carefully remove it from the oven. Allow the cake to cool completely. 6. Enjoy your homemade Easy Bake Oven Vanilla Cake! It's a fantastic treat for kids and a fun way to experiment with baking.

Homemade Chocolate Bliss Brownie

Prep Time: 10 minutes | Cook Time: 15 minutes | Serves: 2

½ cup brownie mix
2 tablespoons water
Non-stick cooking spray
Optional: Mini chocolate chips, chopped nuts, or powdered sugar for garnish

1. Turn on the Easy Bake Oven to preheat it for 15 minutes. 2. Prepare a smooth mixture of brownie mix and water. 3. Grease Oven brownie pan with non-stick cooking spray to avoid sticking. 4. Fill the brownie pan with the mixture and spread it evenly. 5. If you'd like, sprinkle mini chocolate chips or chopped nuts on top of the batter for added flavor and texture. 6. Carefully place the brownie in the Oven. Bake for approximately 12-15 minutes or until the brownies have set and a toothpick inserted into the center comes out clean. Be cautious not to overbake. 7. Once the brownies are done baking, carefully remove them from the oven. Allow the brownies to cool for a few minutes in the pan, then carefully remove them from the pan and place them on a cooling rack.

Chocolate Lava Cake

Prep Time: 10 minutes | Cook Time: 15 minutes | Serves: 2

⅓ cup butter
⅓ cup semi-sweet chocolate chips
¾ cup powdered sugar
2 eggs
6 tablespoons cornstarch

1. Place two greased ramekins on the oven's baking pan. 2. Put the chocolate chips and butter in a microwave-safe bowl and heat in the microwave until melted. 3. Add the sugar and stir well. 4. Add in the eggs and combine until smooth. 5. Add the cornstarch and stir well. 6. Divide the batter between the ramekins. 7. Bake for 15 minutes.

Raspberry Brownies

Prep Time: 15 minutes | Cook Time: 12-15 minutes | Serves: 2-4

¼ cup all-purpose flour
2 tablespoons unsweetened cocoa powder
2 tablespoons granulated sugar
2 tablespoons vegetable oil
2 tablespoons milk
¼ teaspoon vanilla extract
1 tablespoon raspberry jam

1. Preheat your Easy-Bake Oven following the manufacturer's instructions, which usually takes about 15 minutes. 2. Whisk together the flour, granulated sugar and cocoa powder. In another bowl, combine the vegetable oil, milk, and vanilla extract. Mix until well combined. 3. Pour the wet mixture into the dry ingredients and stir until you have a smooth brownie batter. 4. Grease the Easy-Bake Oven pan with a bit of oil or cooking spray. Pour the brownie batter into the greased pan. 5. Drop small spoonfuls of raspberry jam onto the brownie batter. 6. Use a toothpick or a skewer to gently swirl the raspberry jam into the brownie batter to create a marbled effect. Place the pan in the preheated Easy-Bake Oven and bake for approximately 12-15 minutes. 7. Carefully remove the pan from the oven using the spatula and let it cool for a few minutes. Once it's cool enough to handle, remove the brownie from the pan and let it cool completely on a wire rack.

Chocolate Cherry Cake

Prep Time: 10 minutes | Cook Time: 24 minutes | Serves: 3

2 chocolate cake mixes
3 teaspoons water
½ cup cherry pie filling
Whipped cream

1. Plug in your Easy-Bake Ultimate Oven and preheat for 15 minutes. 2. Pour the cake mix from one package into a mixing bowl. 3. Mix until smooth after adding 3 teaspoons of water. 4. Spread the batter in the lined baking pan. 5. Lay the baking pan into the Easy-Bake Ultimate Oven's baking slot. 6. With the help of a pan pusher, push the baking pan into the baking chamber. 7. Adjust the cooking time to 12 minutes and bake. 8. After the cooking time ends, push the baking pan into the cooling chamber with the help of a pan pusher. Allow it to cool for 10 minutes. 9. When cooling is done, with the help of a spatula, remove the baking pan from the oven. 10. While that cake is in the oven, get the second cake mix ready and repeat the baking procedure. 11. Put the cake on a serving plate. 12. Put the cherry pie filling on top of the first layer. 13. Get the second piece of cake from the pan and put it on the cherries. 14. Cherry pie filling should go on top of the second layer. 15. Put whipped cream around the filling and the sides of the cake. Serve and enjoy.

Mini Oreo Brownies

Prep Time: 15 minutes | Cook Time: 15 minutes | Serves: 2-4

¼ cup all-purpose flour
2 tablespoons unsweetened cocoa powder
2 tablespoons granulated sugar
2 tablespoons vegetable oil
2 tablespoons milk
¼ teaspoon vanilla extract
2 Oreo cookies, crushed

1. Preheat your Easy-Bake Oven following the manufacturer's instructions, usually for about 15 minutes. 2. In a small bowl, whisk together the flour, cocoa powder, and granulated sugar. 3. In another bowl, combine the vegetable oil, milk, and vanilla extract. Mix until well combined. 4. Pour the wet mixture into the dry ingredients and stir until you have a smooth brownie batter. 5. Grease the Easy-Bake Oven baking pan with a bit of oil or cooking spray. 6. Pour the brownie batter into the greased pan. 7. Sprinkle the crushed Oreo cookies evenly over the brownie batter. 8. Place the pan in the preheated Easy-Bake Oven and bake for approximately 12-15 minutes. 9. Carefully remove the pan from the oven using the spatula and let it cool for a few minutes. Once it's cool enough to handle, remove the brownie from the pan and let it cool completely on a wire rack.

Mint Chocolate Brownies

Prep Time: 15 minutes | Cook Time: 15 minutes | Serves: 6

2 tablespoons white sugar
Anti-sticking baking spray
2 tablespoons flour, all-purpose
3 tablespoons chocolate syrup
1 tablespoon butter
Frosting:
½ teaspoon peppermint extract
¼ cup confectioners' sugar
½ cup butter

1. Plug in the easy bake oven, preheating it for 15 minutes. 2. Spritz baking spray on the baking pan, followed by dusting with flour. 3. Put sugars and butter into medium-sized bowl and whisk to incorporate. 4. Fold in the chocolate syrup and flour and whisk to incorporate thoroughly. 5. Lay out batter onto the baking pan about 1½-inch apart. 6. Lay out the pan into the "Baking Slot" of Easy-Bake Ultimate Oven. 7. With pan pusher, shove baking pan into the "Baking Chamber". 8. Set the cooking time for 15 minutes. 9. After cooking time is finished, with pan pusher, shove the baking pan into the "Cooling Chamber". 10. Give it about five minutes to cool down. 11. Turn off the oven and with a spatula, take off the baking pan from oven. 12. Cook the remnant cookies in the same way. 13. Merge the frosting ingredients thoroughly and spread over the brownies before enjoying.

Fluffy Banana and Peanut Butter Cake

Prep Time: 10 minutes | Cook Time: 15 minutes | Serves: 2-4

¼ cup all-purpose flour
2 tablespoons granulated sugar
¼ teaspoon baking powder
⅛ teaspoon baking soda
2 tablespoons mashed ripe banana (about half a banana)
2 tablespoons creamy peanut butter
2 tablespoons milk
¼ teaspoon vanilla extract

1. Preheat your easy bake oven for 15 minutes. 2. Whisk together the flour; Sugar, baking powder, and baking soda. 3. In another bowl, combine the mashed banana, peanut butter, milk, and vanilla extract. Stir until well blended. 4. Add the wet mixture to the dry ingredients and stir until you have a smooth batter. 5. Pour the batter into the greased baking pan. 6. Bake in the preheated oven for 12-15 minutes, or until a toothpick inserted into the center comes out clean. 7. Carefully remove the pan from the oven using a spatula and let it cool for a few minutes. 8. Once it's cool enough to handle, remove the cake from the pan and allow it to cool completely on a wire rack.

Colorful Tea Cakes

Prep Time: 15 minutes | Cook Time: 12 minutes | Serves: 8

⅛ teaspoon salt
1 teaspoon multi colored cookie decorations
2 teaspoons sugar
Anti-sticking baking spray
2 teaspoons margarine
¼ teaspoon baking powder
¼ cup flour, all-purpose
4 teaspoons milk

1. Plug in the easy bake oven, preheating it for 15 minutes. 2. Spritz baking spray on the baking pan, followed by dusting with flour. 3. Merge the flour with baking powder, salt, margarine, and sugar to form a crumbly mixture. 4. Gradually incorporate the milk into the mixture, stirring slowly. 5. Sprinkle cookie decorations over the top of each dough portion. 6. Lay small teaspoon-sized portions of the dough onto the baking pan. 7. Bake in the preheated oven for 12 minutes. 8. After cooking time is finished, with pan pusher, shove the baking pan into the "Cooling Chamber". 9. Give it about five minutes to cool down. 10. Then carefully turn the tea cakes onto a platter to serve and enjoy.

Chapter 2 Cookie and Bars Recipes

Coconut Pecan Cookies

Prep Time: 10 minutes | Cook Time: 20 minutes | Serves: 2

½ cup butter
½ cup sugar
1 tablespoon milk
½ teaspoon vanilla
1 ¼ cups all-purpose flour
½ cup finely chopped red candied cherries
¼ cup finely chopped pecans
½ cup coconut flakes

1. Preheat the easy bake oven for 15 minutes. 2. Cream butter and sugar until fluffy. 3. Add milk and vanilla, blending well. 4. Add flour, cherries, and pecans to form stiff dough. 5. Turn onto floured surface and form into an 8" log. 6. Wrap in wax paper and refrigerate 3 hours or overnight. 7. Butter and flour baking pans. 8. Unwrap and slice the dough log into ¼-inch rounds. 9. Place 1 round in the buttered baking pan. 10. Bake until the cookies start to brown around the edges (about 20 minutes). Repeat the cooking steps for the rest round. 11. When cooked, transfer the pan to the cooling chamber and cool for 5 minutes. Then transfer the pan from the oven. Serve and enjoy!

Perfect Thumbprint Cookie

Prep Time: 10 minutes | Cook Time: 12 minutes | Serves: 2

1 tablespoon powdered sugar
2 tablespoons butter
¼ teaspoon vanilla
½ teaspoon water
¼ cup all-purpose flour
Your favorite jelly or jam

1. Preheat the easy bake oven for 15 minutes. 2. Stir together powdered sugar, butter, vanilla, water, and flour until dough forms. 3. Roll the dough between your fingers to make twelve ½-inch balls. 4. Place a few balls at a time on a greased pan with space between them. 5. Press your thumb into the middle of each ball to make a thumb print. 6. Bake in the preheated oven for 10 to 12 minutes. 7. Repeat until all the cookies are baked. 8. When the cookies are cool, fill each thumb print with jam or jelly.

Candied Cherries Nuts Cookies

Prep Time: 10 minutes | Cook Time: 20 minutes | Serves: 4

½ cup softened butter
½ cup packed brown sugar
½ teaspoon vanilla
1½ cups all-purpose flour
1½ teaspoons baking powder
¼ teaspoon salt
3 tablespoons finely chopped candied cherries
3 tablespoons chopped nuts

1. In a bowl, cream butter with sugar and mix in vanilla. 2. In a small bowl, combine flour, baking powder, and salt. 3. Stir the mixture into the butter/sugar mixture. 4. Stir in cherries and nuts. 5. Divide in half. 6. Wrap separately in waxed paper and chill until firm, for about 1 hour. 7. Remove 2 halves from fridge and shape into two 8-inch logs. 8. Wrap again and chill until hard, for about 3 hours or overnight. 9. Unwrap and slice the two logs into ¼" rounds. 10. Place two rounds in the greased baking pan. 11. Bake in the preheated oven for 18 - 20 minutes. 12. Then cool in the cooling chamber for 5 minutes. Enjoy and serve!

White Chocolate Cranberry Cookies

Prep Time: 10 minutes | Cook Time: 10 minutes | Serves: 2

2 tablespoons softened butter
2 tablespoons packed brown sugar
2 tablespoons white sugar
1 teaspoon vanilla extract
¼ cup all-purpose flour
⅛ teaspoon baking soda
3 tablespoons white chocolate chips
¼ cup dried cranberries

1. Preheat the easy bake oven for 15 minutes. 2. Cream the butter and sugars together until smooth. 3. Beat in vanilla extract. 4. In a separate bowl, combine flour and baking soda. 5. Fold into sugar mixture. 6. Mix in white chocolate chips and cranberries. 7. Drop by the teaspoonful onto a buttered baking pan. 8. Bake in the preheated oven for 8 - 10 minutes. 9. Remove to the cooking chamber while still doughy and cool for 5 minutes. 10. Remove from the oven and then serve warm.

Orange Marmalade Oat Bars

Prep Time: 10 minutes | Cook Time: 21 minutes | Serves: 2

1 tablespoon butter, softened
4 teaspoons sugar
⅓ cup flour
4 tablespoons almond milk
⅙ teaspoon baking soda
2 tablespoons quick-cook rolled oats
Dash of salt
5 teaspoons orange marmalade

1. Mix the sugar and butter along with the salt in a bowl until creamy. 2. Add the baking soda, flour, milk, and oats. Mix well. 3. Divide the batter into two prepared baking pans. 4. Press down a little on the mixture. 5. Spread the orange marmalade on the top of each. 6. Bake each for 21 minutes. 7. Once done, let the bars cool completely and then cut into small slices. 8. Serve and enjoy!

Marshmallow Krispie Cereal Treats

Prep Time: 2 minutes | Cook Time: 9 minutes | Serves: 1

1 teaspoon margarine
1 large marshmallow
2 tablespoon rice krispies cereal

1. Plug in your Easy-Bake Ultimate Oven and preheat for 10 minutes. 2. Put marshmallow and margarine in a warming cup that fits the oven, set it on the baking pan, and cover it. 3. Bake in the preheated oven for 9 minutes, stirring well. 4. Fill up another warm cup half way with cereal. In a bowl, mix the cereal well with the hot marshmallow mixture. 5. Use a small amount from the bowl to make the shape of a cookie. Put the shapes on the plate. 6. Put in the fridge for half an hour or until firm.

Chocolate Coconut Oats Bars

Prep Time: 10 minutes | Cook Time: 10 minutes | Serves: 2

¼ cup rolled oats
6 tablespoons coconut flour
⅛ teaspoon baking soda
⅛ teaspoon vanilla extract
2 teaspoons margarine, softened
1 teaspoon white sugar
1 teaspoon brown sugar
1 teaspoon semi-sweet mini chocolate chips
2 teaspoons coconut flakes

1. Mix the rolled oats, coconut flour, baking soda, vanilla extract, margarine, brown sugar, and white sugar in a bowl. 2. Fold in the chocolate chips and coconut flakes. Combine. 3. Press the mixture into the prepared baking pan. 4. Bake for 8 minutes. 5. Let the bar cool for 10 minutes before cutting it into squares. Enjoy!

Homemade Chocolate Granola Bars

Prep Time: 10 minutes | Cook Time: 10 minutes | Serves: 4

¼ cup rolled oats
3 teaspoons all-purpose flour
⅛ teaspoon baking soda
⅛ teaspoon vanilla extract
2 teaspoons butter; softened
1 teaspoon honey
1 teaspoon brown sugar; packed
1 teaspoon mini chocolate chips; semisweet
1 teaspoon raisins

1. Plug in your Easy-Bake Ultimate Oven and preheat for 10 minutes. 2. Mix the first seven ingredients together, then stir in the chocolate chips and raisins. 3. Press mixture gently into Easy-Bake Oven baking pan that has been greased and floured. 4. Lay out the baking pan into the Easy-Bake Ultimate Oven's baking slot. 5. With help of pan pusher, push the baking pan into the baking chamber. 6. Adjust the cooking time to 10 minutes and bake. 7. After the cooking time ends, push the baking pan into the cooling chamber with help of pan pusher. Allow it to cool for 10 minutes. 8. When cooling is done, with help of spatula remove the baking pan from the oven. 9. Cut it into bars. On top of the bar, put vanilla custard and arrange with berries if needed.

Blueberry Danish

Prep Time: 15 minutes | Cook Time: 12 minutes | Serves: 8

¼ cup biscuit mix
½ tablespoon margarine
Anti-sticking baking spray
4 teaspoons milk
¾ teaspoon sugar
½ tablespoon pie filling, blueberry

1. Plug in the easy bake oven, preheating it for 15 minutes. 2. Spritz baking spray on the baking pan, followed by dusting with flour. 3. Merge biscuit mix with margarine and sugar in a bowl and whisk to incorporate into a dough. 4. Divide the dough into small-sized balls. 5. Lay out half of dough balls onto the baking pan about 1½-inch apart. 6. Create an indentation in the center by gently pressing your thumb. 7. Then, fill the indentation with blueberry pie filling. 8. Bake in the preheated oven for 12 minutes. 9. After cooking time is finished, with pan pusher, shove the baking pan into the "Cooling Chamber". 10. Give it about five minutes to cool down. 11. Carefully turn the delicious Danish onto a platter to serve and enjoy.

Delicious Corn Strawberry Bars

Prep Time: 15 minutes | Cook Time: 18 minutes | Serves: 3

Anti-sticking baking spray
1 tablespoon cornflakes, crushed
3 tablespoons flour
1 tablespoon butter, softened
2 teaspoons strawberry jam
1 teaspoon sugar

1. Plug in the easy bake oven, preheating it for 15 minutes. 2. Put flour, cornflakes, butter, and sugar in a bowl and whisk to incorporate coarsely. 3. Reserve 2 tablespoons of mixture and set aside. 4. Lay out residual mixture into the baking pan. 5. Layer the strawberry jam on it. 6. Trickle the reserved mixture over strawberry jam and gently press down. 7. Bake in the preheated oven for 18 minutes. 8. After cooking time is finished, with pan pusher, shove the baking pan into the "Cooling Chamber". 9. Give it about five minutes to cool down. 10. Cut into bars with a sharp knife. Then carefully turn the strawberry bars onto a platter to serve and enjoy.

Classic Butter Cookies

Prep Time: 15 minutes | Cook Time: 5 minutes | Serves: 12

3 teaspoons brown sugar
6 teaspoons butter
¼ cup flour
1 pinch salt
⅛ teaspoon cream of tartar
2 pinches baking soda
Anti-sticking baking spray
3 teaspoons sugar

1. Plug in the easy bake oven, preheating it for 10 minutes. 2. Spritz baking spray on the baking pan, followed by dusting with flour. 3. In a bowl, merge flour with all ingredients until a dough forms. Cut the dough into small equal portions. 4. Portion the cookie dough onto the baking pan about 1½-inch apart. 5. Bake in the preheated oven for 5 minutes. 6. After cooking time is finished, with pan pusher, shove the baking pan into the "Cooling Chamber". 7. Give it about five minutes to cool down. 8. Carefully turn the cookies onto a platter to serve and enjoy.

Corn Apple Bar

Prep Time: 10 minutes | Cook Time: 18 minutes | Serves: 4

3 tablespoons flour
1 tablespoon crushed cornflakes
1 tablespoon soft butter or margarine
1 teaspoon sugar
2 teaspoons apple jelly
⅛ teaspoon cinnamon, optional

1. Plug in your Easy-Bake Ultimate Oven and preheat for 15 minutes. 2. Mix the cornflakes, butter, sugar, cinnamon, and flour in a bowl until the mixture is crumbly. 3. Set aside two tablespoons of the crumbly mix. 4. Firmly press the rest of the mixture into the baking pan. Put jelly on it. Add the crumbled mixture you saved to the jelly and gently press it down with your fingers. 5. Bake in the preheated oven for 18 minutes. 6. After the cooking time ends, push the baking pan into the cooling chamber with the help of a pan pusher. Allow it to cool for 5 minutes. 7. When cooling is done, with the help of spatula, remove the baking pan from the oven. 8. Cut them into squares and enjoy.

Chocolate Chip Peanut Butter Cookies

Prep Time: 10 minutes | Cook Time: 20 minutes | Serves: 12

Anti-sticking baking spray
¼ cup peanut butter
¼ cup sugar
2¼ teaspoons egg, beaten
¼ teaspoon vanilla extract
1 tablespoon mini chocolate chips
1 tablespoon walnuts, chopped

1. Preheat your Easy-Bake Ultimate Oven for 15 minutes. 2. Spray the baking pan with baking spray and then dust it lightly with flour. 3. Put peanut butter and remnant ingredients into a bowl and blend to incorporate thoroughly. 4. Divide the dough into small-sized balls. 5. Lay out the dough balls onto the prepared baking pan about 1½-inch apart and flatten out. 6. Bake in the preheated oven for 20 minutes. 7. Cook the remnant cookies in the same way. 8. Shift the baking pan onto a counter to cool for around 5 minutes. 9. Carefully turn the cookies onto a platter to cool thoroughly before enjoying.

Chocolate Graham Cracker Cookies

Prep Time: 4 minutes | Cook Time: 5 minutes | Serves: 2

1 tablespoon peanut butter
1 pack graham crackers
2 teaspoon mini chocolate chips

1. Plug in your Easy-Bake Ultimate Oven and preheat for 15 minutes. 2. Add a little peanut butter to the graham cracker. 3. Add chocolate chips on top. Place it on the baking pan. 4. Bake in the preheated oven for 5 minutes. 5. After the cooking time ends, push the baking pan into the cooling chamber with the help of a pan pusher. Allow it to cool for 5 minutes. 6. When cooling is done, with the help of spatula, remove the baking pan from the oven. 7. Take the cookies out and spread it out. 8. Let the cookies cool down a bit before you eat it.

Strawberry Bars

Prep Time: 10 minutes | Cook Time: 18 minutes | Serves: 2

3 tablespoons flour
1 tablespoon cornflakes; crushed
1 tablespoon butter or margarine; softened
1 teaspoon sugar
2 teaspoons strawberry jam

1. Plug in your Easy-Bake Ultimate Oven and preheat for 15 minutes. 2. Crumble the grains, butter, and sugar together with flour. 3. Set aside 2 tablespoons of the mixture. 4. Firmly press the rest of the mixture into the Easy-Bake Oven baking pan. Put jam on it. 5. Sprinkle the crumble you saved over the jam and gently press it down. 6. Bake in the preheated oven for 18 minutes. 7. After the cooking time ends, push the baking pan into the cooling chamber with the help of a pan pusher. Allow it to cool for 5 minutes. 8. When cooling is done, with the help of spatula, remove the baking pan from the oven.

Easy Sugar Cookies

Prep Time: 10 minutes | Cook Time: 20 minutes | Serves: 16

Anti-sticking baking spray
6 teaspoons butter
3 teaspoons sugar
3 teaspoons brown sugar
1 pinch of salt
¼ cup all-purpose flour
⅛ teaspoon baking powder
⅛ teaspoon vanilla extract

1. Preheat your Easy-Bake Ultimate Oven for 15 minutes. 2. Spray the baking pan with baking spray and then dust it lightly with flour. 3. Put butter, sugars and salt into a large bowl and whisk to form a creamy mixture. 4. Put in remnant ingredients and whisk to form a soft dough. 5. Divide the dough into small-sized balls. 6. Lay out the dough balls onto the prepared baking pan about 1½-inch apart. 7. Bake in the preheated oven for 20 minutes. 8. Cook the remnant cookies in the same way. 9. Shift the baking pan onto a counter to cool for around 5 minutes. 10. Carefully turn the cookies onto a platter to cool thoroughly before enjoying.

Lemon Sunshine Cookies

Prep Time: 10 minutes | Cook Time: 15 minutes | Serves: 4

For the Cookies:
¼ cup (½ stick) unsalted butter, softened
¼ cup granulated sugar
1 small egg
½ teaspoon lemon zest (from 1 lemon)
½ teaspoon lemon juice
1 cup all-purpose flour
¼ teaspoon baking powder
A pinch of salt

For the Lemon Glaze:
½ cup powdered sugar
1 tablespoon lemon juice
Yellow food coloring (optional, for a sunny glaze)

1. In a mixing bowl, cream together the softened butter and granulated sugar until well combined. Also preheat your Easy Bake Oven according to the manufacturer's instructions. 2. Beat in the small egg, lemon zest, and lemon juice, mixing until smooth and fragrant. 3. In a separate bowl, whisk together the all-purpose flour, baking powder, and a pinch of salt. Gradually add the dry ingredient mixture to the wet ingredients, stirring until a dough forms. 4. Roll small portions of the dough into sunshine-shaped cookies or any fun shapes using your hands or cookie cutters. 5. Place the shaped cookies on the parchment paper-lined baking pan. Bake in the Easy Bake Oven for around 15 minutes. 6. Meanwhile, prepare the lemon glaze by mixing the powdered sugar and lemon juice. Add a few drops of yellow food coloring for a sunny glaze, if desired. 7. Once the cookies are done and have cooled for a few minutes, drizzle or spread the lemon glaze over the top of each cookie. 8. Allow the glaze to set, and let the cookies cool completely on a wire rack.

Milk Chocolate Chip Cookies

Prep Time: 10 minutes | Cook Time: 15 minutes | Serves: 12

Anti-sticking baking spray
6 teaspoons all-purpose flour
3 teaspoons sugar
⅛ teaspoon baking soda
4 teaspoons milk
1½ teaspoons butter, softened
⅛ teaspoon vanilla extract
12-15 chocolate chips

1. Preheat your Easy-Bake Ultimate Oven for 15 minutes. 2. Spray the baking pan with baking spray and then dust it lightly with flour. 3. Put flour, baking soda and sugar into a bowl and blend thoroughly. 4. Put milk, butter and vanilla extract into another bowl and whisk-incorporate. 5. Put milk mixture into flour mixture and blend to form like a thick cookie dough. Gently blend in chocolate. 6. Divide the dough into small-sized balls. 7. Lay out the dough balls onto the prepared baking pan about 1½-inch apart and flatten out. 8. Bake in the preheated oven for 15 minutes. 9. After cooking time is finished, with a pan pusher, push the "Baking Pan" into the "Cooling Chamber". Let it cool for around 5 minutes. 10. Turn off the oven and with a spatula, take off the "Baking Pan" from oven. 11. Cook the remnant cookies in the same way. 12. Shift the baking pan onto a counter to cool for around 5 minutes. 13. Carefully turn the cookies onto a platter to cool thoroughly before enjoying.

Chocolate Oats Cookies

Prep Time: 10 minutes | Cook Time: 10-12 minutes | Serves: 4

1½ cups quick cooking oats
¾ cup all-purpose flour
¼ teaspoon baking soda
¾ cup brown sugar; packed
½ cup shortening
1 tablespoon raisins; optional
1 tablespoon semisweet chocolate chips; mini, optional
Sugar

1. Plug in your Easy-Bake Ultimate Oven and preheat for 15 minutes. 2. Add the oats, flour, baking soda, and brown sugar to a medium-sized bowl. Mix it up. Using a pastry blender, cut in the shortening until the mixture looks like corn meal. Set the mixture aside. Put chocolate chips and raisins in it. 3. Using a spoon, mix the ingredients together until they stick together in a big ball. Make a ball out of one teaspoon of dough at a time. 4. Place in the baking pan that hasn't been greased. Grease the bottom of a small glass. 5. Put sugar on the bottom of a glass that has been toasted. Press each ball down with a sugar-coated glass to make it flat. 6. Bake in the preheated oven for 10-12 minutes. 7. After the cooking time ends, push the baking pan into the cooling chamber with the help of a pan pusher. Allow it to cool for 5 minutes. 8. When cooling is done, with the help of spatula, remove the baking pan from the oven.

Cream Cheese Cookies

Prep Time: 10 minutes | Cook Time: 10 minutes | Serves: 3

2 tablespoons butter; softened
2 tablespoons cream cheese; softened
⅛ teaspoon salt
⅛ teaspoon almond extract
⅛ teaspoon vanilla extract
¼ cup and 2 tablespoons all-purpose flour

1. Plug in your Easy-Bake Ultimate Oven and preheat for 15 minutes. 2. Add everything but the flour and beat until the mixture is smooth. Add the flour and mix it in well. Leave to chill overnight. 3. Roll out the dough to a thickness of ⅛ inch on a lightly floured surface. 4. Put the extra dough in the fridge until you're ready to use it. 5. Use lightly floured cookie tools to cut the dough into the shapes you want and place the cookie dough in the baking pan. 6. Bake in the preheated oven for 7-10 minutes. 7. After the cooking time ends, push the baking pan into the cooling chamber with the help of a pan pusher. Allow it to cool for 5 minutes. 8. When cooling is done, with the help of spatula, remove the baking pan from the oven. 9. Let cookies cool all the way down before frosting them.

Butter Cheese Twists

Prep Time: 10 minutes | Cook Time: 15 minutes | Serves: 4

8-ounce can refrigerator crescent rolls
2 teaspoons butter; melted
½ cup cheese; grated
Garlic salt

1. Plug in your Easy-Bake Ultimate Oven and preheat for 15 minutes. 2. Cut the roll dough into two parts. Make two squares. Press the holes to close them. 3. Butter the first square, then add cheese and garlic salt. 4. Put the second piece of dough on top of the first one. 5. Slice into ½-inch pieces. Five times, twist each strip. Squeeze the ends to close. 6. Place on a baking pan that has been oiled. 7. Lay out the baking pan into the Easy-Bake Ultimate Oven's baking slot. 8. With help of pan pusher, push the baking pan into the baking chamber. 9. Adjust the cooking time to 15 minutes and bake until golden brown. 10. After the cooking time ends, push the baking pan into the cooling chamber with help of pan pusher. Allow it to cool for 5 minutes. 11. When cooling is done, with the help of spatula remove the baking pan from the oven. 12. Serve and enjoy.

Herb-Butter Glazed Cheese Biscuits

Prep Time: 10 minutes | Cook Time: 15 minutes | Serves: 4

½ cup baking mix
2 tablespoons plus
teaspoon 2 milk
2 tablespoons shredded
cheddar cheese
1 tablespoon parmesan
cheese
For the Glaze:
1 tablespoon butter
⅛ garlic powder
¼ teaspoon dried
parsley

1. Plug in your Easy-Bake Ultimate Oven and preheat for 15 minutes. 2. Stir baking mix, milk, and cheeses until they form a soft dough. 3. Drop by spoonful on a baking pan that hasn't been oiled. 4. Lay out the baking pan into the Easy-Bake Ultimate Oven's baking slot. 5. With help of pan pusher, push the baking pan into the baking chamber. 6. Adjust the cooking time to 15 minutes and bake or until the bottoms are lightly browned. 7. After the cooking time ends, push the baking pan into the cooling chamber with the help of pan pusher. Allow it to cool for 5 minutes. 8. When cooling is done, with the help of spatula remove the baking pan from the oven. 9. Melt the butter in a micro-safe bowl and mix in the garlic powder and parsley flakes. 10. Coat the garlic butter on warm biscuits with a brush. Serve and enjoy.

Almond Chocolate Coconut Cookies

Prep Time: 15 minutes | Cook Time: 8-10 minutes | Serves: 2-4

¼ cup all-purpose flour
2 tablespoons granulated sugar
2 tablespoons shredded coconut
1 tablespoon chopped almonds
2 tablespoons chocolate chips
2 tablespoons vegetable oil
¼ teaspoon almond extract
¼ teaspoon vanilla extract

1. Preheat your easy bake oven for 15 minutes. 2. In a small bowl, combine the flour, granulated sugar, shredded coconut, chopped almonds, and chocolate chips. 3. In another bowl, combine the vegetable oil, almond extract, and vanilla extract. Mix well. 4. Pour the wet mixture into the dry ingredients and stir until you have a cohesive cookie dough. 5. Roll the cookie dough into small balls and place them on a greased Easy-Bake Oven baking pan. Make sure to space them apart. 6. Gently flatten each cookie with your fingers or the back of a fork. 7. Place the baking pan in the preheated Easy-Bake Oven and bake for approximately 8-10 minutes or until the cookies are lightly golden brown around the edges. 8. Carefully remove the cookies from the oven using the spatula and let them cool for a few minutes. Once they're cool enough to handle, transfer them to a wire rack to cool completely.

Crunchy Lemon Blueberry Cookies

Prep Time: 15 minutes | Cook Time: 8-10 minutes | Serves: 2-4

¼ cup all-purpose flour
2 tablespoons granulated sugar
⅛ teaspoon baking powder
⅛ teaspoon baking soda
Zest of half a lemon
1 tablespoon lemon juice
2 tablespoons vegetable oil
¼ teaspoon vanilla extract
1 tablespoon fresh or frozen blueberries

1. Preheat your Easy-Bake Oven for about 15 minutes. 2. Whisk together the flour, granulated sugar, baking powder, baking soda, and lemon zest. In another bowl, combine the lemon juice, vegetable oil, and vanilla extract. Mix well. 3. Pour the wet mixture into the dry ingredients and stir until you have a smooth cookie dough. 4. Gently fold in the fresh or frozen blueberries into the cookie dough. 5. Roll cookie dough into small balls and place them on a greased Easy-Bake Oven baking pan. Make sure to space them apart. 6. Use a fork or your fingers to gently flatten each cookie. 7. Place the baking pan in the preheated Easy-Bake Oven and bake for approximately 8-10 minutes or until the edges of the cookies are light golden brown.8. Carefully remove the cookies from the oven using the spatula and let them cool for a few minutes. Once they're cool enough to handle, transfer them to a wire rack to cool completely.

Tasty Pecan Cookies

Prep Time: 15 minutes | Cook Time: 8-10 minutes | Serves: 2-4

¼ cup all-purpose flour
2 tablespoons granulated sugar
⅛ teaspoon baking powder
⅛ teaspoon baking soda
2 tablespoons chopped pecans
2 tablespoons vegetable oil
1 tablespoon maple syrup
¼ teaspoon vanilla extract

1. Preheat your easy bake oven for 15 minutes. 2. In a small bowl, whisk together the flour, granulated sugar, baking powder, and baking soda. 3. Stir in the chopped pecans into the dry ingredients. 4. Combine the vegetable oil, maple syrup, and vanilla extract. Mix well. Pour the wet mixture into the dry ingredients and stir until you have a smooth cookie dough. 5. Roll the cookie dough into small balls and place them on a greased Easy-Bake Oven baking pan. Make sure to space them apart. Use a fork or your fingers to gently flatten each cookie. 6. Place the baking pan in the preheated Easy-Bake Oven and bake for approximately 8-10 minutes or until the cookies are lightly golden brown around the edges. Keep an eye on them, as cooking times may vary depending on your Easy-Bake Oven. 7. Carefully remove the cookies from the oven using the spatula and let them cool for a few minutes. Once they're cool enough to handle, transfer them to a wire rack to cool completely.

Peanut Butter Chocolate Cookies

Prep Time: 10 minutes | Cook Time: 7 minutes | Serves: 4

¼ cup (½ stick) unsalted butter, softened
¼ cup granulated sugar
¼ cup firmly packed brown sugar
¼ cup creamy peanut butter
1 small egg
¾ cup all-purpose flour
¼ teaspoon baking soda
A pinch of salt
12 small chocolate candy kisses (e.g., Hershey's Kisses)

1. Preheat the easy bake oven for 15 minutes. 2. Cream together the softened butter, brown sugar, granulated sugar, and creamy peanut butter until well combined and creamy. Add the small egg to the mixture and mix until smooth. 3. Gradually mix the dry ingredients and add that mixture to the wet ingredients, stirring until well combined. 4. Roll the cookie dough into small balls, about the size of a marble. 5. Place the cookie dough balls on the parchment paper-lined baking pan. Bake in the Easy Bake Oven for around 5-7 minutes. 6. As soon as the cookies come out of the oven, press one chocolate candy kiss into the center of each cookie while they are still warm. 7. Let the cookies cool for a few minutes to set the chocolate. 8. Enjoy your freshly baked Peanut Butter Blossom Cookies from your Easy Bake Oven.

Rainbow Butter Cookies

Prep Time: 10 minutes | Cook Time: 7 minutes | Serves: 4

¼ cup (½ stick) unsalted butter, softened
¼ cup granulated sugar
1 small egg
½ teaspoon vanilla extract
1 cup all-purpose flour
¼ teaspoon baking powder
A pinch of salt
Food coloring

1. Preheat the easy bake oven for 15 minutes. 2. Beat in the small egg and vanilla extract, mixing until smooth. Also, cream together the softened butter and granulated sugar until well combined. 3. In a separate bowl, whisk together the all-purpose flour, baking powder, and a pinch of salt. 4. Gradually add the dry ingredient mixture to the wet ingredients, stirring until a soft dough forms. 5. Divide the cookie dough into smaller portions (one for each color you want to use). 6. Add a few drops of different food coloring to each portion of dough. Knead the dough until the color is evenly distributed. 7. Shape each colored dough into small balls or fun shapes using your hands or cookie cutters. 8. Place the shaped cookies on the parchment paper-lined baking pan. Bake in the Easy Bake Oven for around 5-7 minutes. 9. Allow the cookies to cool for a few minutes on a wire rack.

Best S'mores Cookies

Prep Time: 15 minutes | Cook Time: 8-10 minutes | Serves: 2-4

¼ cup all-purpose flour
2 tablespoons graham cracker crumbs
2 tablespoons granulated sugar
⅛ teaspoon baking powder
⅛ teaspoon baking soda
2 tablespoons unsalted butter, softened
¼ teaspoon vanilla extract
1 tablespoon mini chocolate chips
1 tablespoon mini marshmallows

1. Preheat your easy bake oven for 15 minutes. 2. In a small bowl, whisk together the flour, graham cracker crumbs, granulated sugar, baking powder, and baking soda. 3. Add the softened butter and vanilla extract to the dry ingredients. Mix until you have a crumbly cookie dough. 4. Gently fold in the mini chocolate chips and mini marshmallows into the cookie dough. 5. Roll the cookie dough into small balls, about ½ inch in size. Place them on a greased Easy-Bake Oven baking pan, spacing them slightly apart. 6. Use the back of a spoon or your fingers to gently flatten each cookie. 7. Place the baking pan in the preheated Easy-Bake Oven and bake for approximately 8-10 minutes or until the cookies are lightly golden brown. Keep an eye on them, as cooking times may vary depending on your Easy-Bake Oven. 8. Carefully remove the cookies from the oven using the spatula and let them cool for a few minutes. Once they're cool enough to handle, transfer them to a wire rack to cool completely.

Chapter 3 Snack and Dessert Recipes

Cheese Apple Slices

Prep Time: 5 minutes | Cook Time: 15 minutes | Serves: 2

¼ teaspoon butter
1 large apple
2 tablespoons shredded cheddar cheese

1. Preheat the easy bake oven for 15 minutes. 2. Wash the apple and remove its center core. 3. Slice across the apple to make rings about ½ inch thick. 4. Butter a baking pan. 5. Place apple slices in pan one at a time. Add cheese. 6. Bake each slice for about 15 minutes.

Cheese Ham Bagels

Prep Time: 15 minutes | Cook Time: 15 minutes | Serves: 2

1 slice deli ham
Anti-sticking baking spray
1 bagel, halved
4 tablespoons cheddar cheese

1. Plug in the easy bake oven, preheating it for 15 minutes. 2. Spritz baking spray on the baking pan, followed by dusting with flour. 3. Position a slice of ham onto a toasted bagel half. 4. In each of the warming cups of Easy-Bake Oven, divide the cheese. 5. Warm the cheese in a small microwave-safe bowl. 6. Trickle the warm cheese over the ham slice on the bagel. 7. Top the sandwich with the other toasted bagel half and assemble it. 8. Lay out sandwiches onto the baking pan. 9. Bake in the preheated oven for15 minutes. 10. After cooking time is finished, with pan pusher, shove the baking pan into the "Cooling Chamber". 11. Give it about five minutes to cool down. 12. Carefully turn the bagels onto a platter to serve and enjoy.

Cheesy Hot Dogs with Mashed Potatoes

Prep Time: 10 minutes | Cook Time: 15 minutes | Serves: 2

2 hot dogs
½ cup mashed potatoes
½ cup cheddar or
parmesan cheese; grated

1. Plug in your Easy-Bake Ultimate Oven and preheat for 10 minutes. 2. Cut three slits in the hot dog lengthwise and place in the baking pan. 3. Put mashed potatoes in the split hole. Add cheese on top. 4. Bake in the preheated oven for 15 minutes. 5. After the cooking time ends, allow it to cool for 5 minutes and serve.

Chocolate Ice Cream Sandwich Bars

Prep Time: 15 minutes | Cook Time: 20 minutes | Serves: 2

Cake:
6 tablespoons chocolate
cake box mix
3 tablespoons hot water
1½ tablespoons egg
(beaten)
1½ teaspoon butter
(softened)
¼ teaspoon vanilla
extract
Center Filling
½ - ¾ cup vanilla ice
cream (softened)

1. Preheat the easy bake oven for 15 minutes. Spray a baking pan with nonstick spray. 2. Combine all of the cake ingredients together in a small bowl. 3. Divide batter into 2 servings and place one at a time to the prepared baking pan. 4. Bake each for 10-12 minutes or until cake pulls away from sides. 5. Remove pan from oven and allow cake to cool completely. 6. Spread ice cream over top of cake 1. Layer cake 2 on top to form an ice cream sandwich cake. 7. Place in a freezer until the ice cream is frozen. 8. Slice into bars and serve immediately.

Cinnamon Apple Slices

Prep Time: 5 minutes | Cook Time: 20 minutes | Serves: 2

1 large apple
¼ teaspoon butter
⅛ teaspoon cinnamon
1 tablespoon sugar

1. Preheat the easy bake oven for 15 minutes. 2. Wash a large apple and remove its center core. 3. Slice across the apple to make ½" thick rings. 4. Butter a baking pan. 5. Place apple slice(s) in pan one at a time. 6. Sprinkle lightly with cinnamon. 7. Sprinkle lightly with sugar. Top with butter. 8. Bake for about 20 minutes.

Delicious Cheese Hot Dog Crackers

Prep Time: 15 minutes | Cook Time: 8 minutes | Serves: 8

2 squares American cheese, sliced into 4 squares
1 hot dog, cut into 8 slices
8 Ritz Crackers

1. Plug in the easy bake oven, preheating it for 15 minutes. 2. Position one square of cheese on each cracker, and then place a slice of hot dog on top. 3. Lay out crackers onto the baking pan. 4. Bake in the preheated oven for 8 minutes. 5. After cooking time is finished, with pan pusher, shove the baking pan into the "Cooling Chamber". 6. Give it about five minutes to cool down. 7. Carefully turn the crackers onto a platter to serve and enjoy.

Red Velvet Ice Cream Sandwich Bars

Prep Time: 15 minutes | Cook Time: 20 minutes | Serves: 2

Cake:
6 tablespoons red velvet cake box mix
3 tablespoons hot water
1 ½ tablespoons applesauce or egg (beaten)
1 ½ teaspoon butter (softened)
¼ teaspoon vanilla extract
Center Filling
½ - ¾ cup vanilla ice cream (softened)

1. Preheat the easy bake oven for 15 minutes. Spray a baking pan with nonstick spray. 2. Mix all cake ingredients together in a small bowl. 3. Divide the batter into 2 servings and then place one at a time to the pan. 4. Bake each for 10-12 minutes or until the cake pulls away from sides. 5. Allow the cake to cool completely and then remove it from the oven. 6. Spread the vanilla ice cream over top of cake 1. Layer cake 2 on top to form an ice cream sandwich cake. 7. Place in a freezer until the ice cream is frozen. 8. Slice into bars and serve immediately.

Strawberry Ice Cream Sandwich Bars

Prep Time: 15 minutes | Cook Time: 20 minutes | Serves: 2

Cake:
6 tablespoons strawberry cake box mix
3 tablespoons milk
1 ½ tablespoons egg (beaten)
1 ½ teaspoon butter (softened)
¼ teaspoon vanilla extract
Center Filling
½ - ¾ cup vanilla ice cream (softened)

1. Preheat the easy bake oven for 15 minutes. Spray the pan with nonstick spray. 2. Mix all cake ingredients together in a small bowl. 3. Divide the batter into 2 servings and place one at a time to the baking pan. 4. Bake each for 10-12 minutes or until the cake pulls away from sides. 5. Allow the cake to cool completely and then remove from the oven. 6. Spread ice cream over top of cake 1. Layer cake 2 on top to form an ice cream sandwich cake. 7. Place the sandwich in a freezer until the ice cream is frozen. 8. Slice into bars and serve immediately.

Simple Cornbread

Prep Time: 15 minutes | Cook Time: 15 minutes | Serves: 6

2 teaspoons butter
2 tablespoons milk
Anti-sticking baking spray
1 tablespoon sugar
½ teaspoon baking soda
¼ cup flour, all-purpose
¼ teaspoon vanilla extract
1 tablespoon cornmeal

1. Plug in the easy bake oven, preheating it for 15 minutes. 2. Begin by dividing the dry and wet ingredients into separate bowls. 3. Merge both sets of ingredients in their respective bowls, then gradually merge the dry and wet ingredients. 4. While adding wet ingredients, continue to mix the mixture thoroughly. 5. Grease the baking pan with the baking spray. Lay out the mixture onto the baking pan about 1½-inch apart. 6. Bake in the preheated oven for 15 minutes. 7. After cooking time is finished, shift the baking pan on a countertop to cool down for approximately five minutes. 8. Carefully turn the cornbread onto a platter to serve and enjoy.

Homemade Caramel Popcorn Balls

Prep Time: 5 minutes | Cook Time: 10 minutes | Serves: 1

4 tablespoon caramel syrup, candy or topping
½ cup popped unsalted popcorn

1. Plug in your Easy-Bake Ultimate Oven and preheat for 10 minutes. 2. Place the caramel syrup in a small baking cup that fits the oven. Place the cup in the baking pan. 3. Bake in the preheated oven for about 10 minutes. 4. Then stir well and pour the warm sauce over the popcorn. 5. Make a ball out of the popcorn using hands that are lightly greased. 6. Put plastic wrap around it. 7. Put in the fridge until firm. Serve and enjoy.

Cheese Nachos

Prep Time: 10 minutes | Cook Time: 8-10 minutes | Serves: 1

1 pack tortilla chips
½ cup bean dip
½ cup grated cheese

1. Plug in your Easy-Bake Ultimate Oven and preheat for 10 minutes. 2. Put tortilla chips on the baking pan. 3. Grate the cheese and bean dip over the top. 4. Bake in the preheated oven for 8-10 minutes. 5. After the cooking time ends, push the baking pan into the cooling chamber with the help of a pan pusher. Allow it to cool for 5 minutes. 6. When cooling is done, with the help of spatula, remove the baking pan from the oven.

BBQ Cheese Chicken Pizza

Prep Time: 10 minutes | Cook Time: 20 minutes | Serves: 1

Anti-sticking baking spray
2 tablespoons all-purpose flour
⅛ teaspoon baking soda
1 pinch of salt
1 teaspoon margarine
1 tablespoon BBQ Sauce
2 tablespoons chicken
1½ tablespoons mozzarella cheese, shredded

1. Preheat your Easy-Bake Ultimate Oven for 15 minutes. 2. Spray an Easy-Bake Oven baking pan with baking spray. 3. Put the flour, baking soda, salt, and butter into a bowl and whisk to form a dough. Shape the dough into a ball. 4. Lay out the dough ball into the center of prepared pan. 5. With your hands, pat the dough slightly to cover the bottom and halfway up the sides of pan. 6. Spread the BBQ Sauce over the dough and top with chicken, followed by the cheese. 7. Bake in the preheated oven for 20 minutes. 8. After cooking time is finished, with a pan pusher, push the "Baking Pan" into the "Cooling Chamber". Let it cool for around 5 minutes. 9. Turn off the oven and with a spatula, take off the "Baking Pan" from oven. 10. Shift the pizza pan onto a counter to cool for around 5 minutes. 11. Enjoy moderately hot.

Garlic Butter Biscuits

Prep Time: 10 minutes | Cook Time: 10 minutes | Serves: 6

Anti-sticking baking spray
¼ cup of Bisquick mix
4 teaspoons milk
1 tablespoon butter, melted
⅛ teaspoon garlic powder
¼ teaspoon dried parsley

1. Preheat your Easy-Bake Ultimate Oven for 15 minutes. 2. Spray an Easy-Bake Oven baking pan with baking spray. 3. Put Bisquick and milk into a bowl and with a fork, blend to incorporate. 4. Lay out the mixture onto the prepared pan about 1½-inch apart. 5. Bake in the preheated oven for 10 minutes. 6. After cooking time is finished, with a pan pusher, push the "Baking Pan" into the "Cooling Chamber". Let it cool for around 5 minutes. 7. Turn off the oven and with a spatula, take off the "Baking Pan" from oven. 8. Transfer the baking pan of biscuits onto a counter to cool for around 5 minutes. 9. Meanwhile, put butter, garlic powder and parsley in a bowl and blend to incorporate. 10. Brush the top of warm biscuits with butter mixture and enjoy.

Mini Cheese Pizza Bagels

Prep Time: 10 minutes | Cook Time: 10 minutes | Serves: 2-4

2 mini bagels, split in half
4 tablespoons pizza sauce
½ cup shredded mozzarella cheese
Your choice of toppings (e.g., mini pepperoni slices, sliced olives, diced bell peppers, etc.)

1. Place the split mini bagels in the baking pan. Spread 1 tablespoon of pizza sauce on each bagel half. 2. Sprinkle a generous amount of shredded mozzarella cheese on top of the sauce. Add your choice of toppings to each bagel half. Get creative with your favorite pizza toppings. 3. Carefully place the prepared mini pizza bagels in the Easy-Bake Oven. Bake for approximately 8-10 minutes, or until the cheese is melted and bubbly, and the bagels are lightly toasted. 4. Carefully remove the mini pizza bagels from the oven using the spatula. Let them cool for a minute or two before enjoying your delicious homemade snack.

Peanut Butter Candies

Prep Time: 5 minutes | Cook Time: 15 minutes | Serves: 1

¼ cup peanut butter chips
2 teaspoons margarine

1. Plug in your Easy-Bake Ultimate Oven and preheat for 10 minutes. 2. Place the peanut butter chips and margarine in the baking pan. 3. Bake in the preheated oven for 15 minutes until they are melted. Slowly stir well. 4. Use a spoon to fill the candy moulds with the melted mixture. 5. For 30 minutes or until firm, put the moulds in the fridge. 6. Take out of the moulds and serve.

Balsamic Caprese Skewers

Prep Time: 10 minutes | Cook Time: 4 minutes | Serves: 2-4

Cherry tomatoes
Mini mozzarella cheese balls (bocconcini)
Fresh basil leaves
Extra-virgin olive oil
Balsamic glaze (store-bought or homemade)
Salt and pepper to taste
Mini skewers or toothpicks

1. Wash the cherry tomatoes and basil leaves. Drain the mini mozzarella cheese balls if needed. 2. Thread one cherry tomato, one mozzarella cheese ball, and one fresh basil leaf onto each mini skewer or toothpick. Repeat until you have as many skewers as desired. 3. Drizzle extra-virgin olive oil over the assembled skewers, and lightly season them with salt and pepper to taste. 4. Preheat your Easy-Bake Oven following the manufacturer's instructions, typically for about 15 minutes. Carefully place the assembled Caprese skewers in the baking pan. 5. Bake in the preheated oven for approximately 3-4 minutes, or until the cheese begins to soften and the tomatoes become slightly blistered. 6. Remove the Caprese skewers from the oven using the spatula. Drizzle them with balsamic glaze for added flavor. 7. Allow the skewers to cool slightly before enjoying your mini Caprese skewers.

Mini Veggie Pita Pizzas

Prep Time: 15 minutes | Cook Time: 8-10 minutes | Serves: 2-4

2 mini whole wheat pita bread rounds
4 tablespoons tomato sauce or pizza sauce
½ cup shredded mozzarella cheese
Your choice of fresh vegetables (e.g., sliced bell peppers, cherry tomatoes, sliced olives, thinly sliced mushrooms)
Dried Italian herbs (optional, for seasoning)
Olive oil (for brushing)

1. Carefully split the mini pita bread rounds in half to create four thin pita pockets. 2. Place the pita pockets on a clean surface or a small baking sheet. Spread 1 tablespoon of tomato or pizza sauce inside each pita pocket. 3. Sprinkle a generous amount of shredded mozzarella cheese inside each pita pocket. Add your choice of fresh vegetables on top of the cheese. Get creative with your veggie combinations. 4. If desired, sprinkle a pinch of dried Italian herbs over the vegetables for added flavor. Lightly brush the outer sides of the pita pockets with olive oil. 5. Carefully place the assembled mini veggie pita pizzas in the Easy-Bake Oven baking pan. Bake for approximately 8-10 minutes or until the cheese is melted, and the pita bread is lightly toasted. 6. Remove the mini veggie pita pizzas from the oven using the spatula. Let them cool for a minute or two before enjoying your delicious and customizable snack.

Bacon Cheddar Potato Skins

Prep Time: 10 minutes | Cook Time: 30 minutes | Serves: 2-4

2 small russet potatoes
¼ cup shredded cheddar cheese
2 strips of cooked bacon, crumbled
2 tablespoons sour cream
Chopped fresh chives or green onions (optional, for garnish)
Salt and pepper to taste

1. Preheat your easy bake oven for 15 minutes. 2. Wash and scrub the potatoes thoroughly. Pierce them several times with a fork to allow steam to escape during baking. 3. Place the potatoes directly in the baking pan in your Easy-Bake Oven. Bake for approximately 25-30 minutes, or until the potatoes are tender when pierced with a fork. 4. Carefully remove the baked potatoes from the oven using the spatula. Allow them to cool slightly, then cut each potato in half lengthwise. 5. Use a spoon to scoop out some of the potato flesh from each half, leaving a thin layer of potato attached to the skin. Reserve the scooped-out potato for another use. 6. Sprinkle shredded cheddar cheese and crumbled bacon evenly over the potato skins. 7. Place the loaded potato skins in the baking pan. Bake for an additional 3-5 minutes, or until the cheese is melted and bubbly. 8. Remove the mini baked potato skins from the oven using the spatula. Season with salt and pepper to taste. 9. Top each with a small dollop of sour cream and garnish with chopped fresh chives or green onions if desired.

Crispy Cheese Twists

Prep Time: 15 minutes | Cook Time: 15 minutes | Serves: 12

Anti-sticking baking spray
3 teaspoons butter, melted
¾ cup cheese, grated
12-ounce can refrigerator crescent rolls
Garlic salt, to taste

1. Plug in the easy bake oven, preheating it for 15 minutes. 2. Spritz baking spray on the baking pan, followed by dusting with flour. 3. Split the dough into two portions and flatten them into rectangular shapes. 4. Seal any perforations by pressing them together. 5. Next, brush butter on the surface of first rectangle and then dash it with garlic salt and cheese. 6. Position the second dough rectangle on top of the first one at this point.7. Slice the dough into strips that are approximately ½ inch wide. 8. Twist each strip five times, and then firmly pinch the ends together to seal them. 9. Lay out twisted dough strips onto the baking pan about 1½-inch apart. 10. Bake in the preheated oven for 15 minutes. 11. After cooking time is finished, with pan pusher, shove the baking pan into the "Cooling Chamber". 12. Give it about five minutes to cool down. 13. Carefully turn the cheese twists onto a platter to serve and enjoy.

Butter Cheese Breadsticks
Prep Time: 10 minutes | Cook Time: 8-10 minutes | Serves: 2-4

For the Breadstick Dough:
½ cup all-purpose flour
½ teaspoon baking powder
¼ teaspoon salt
¼ cup milk
1 tablespoon vegetable oil
For the Topping:
2 tablespoons melted butter
¼ teaspoon garlic powder
2 tablespoons grated Parmesan cheese
Chopped fresh parsley

1. In a small bowl, whisk together the flour, baking powder, and salt. Add the milk and vegetable oil, and stir until a soft dough forms. 2. Divide the dough into two equal portions. Roll each portion into a thin rope or breadstick shape. Place them on a greased Easy-Bake Oven baking pan. 3. Place the baking pan in the preheated Easy-Bake Oven and bake for approximately 8-10 minutes, or until the breadsticks are lightly golden brown. Keep a close eye on them, as cooking times may vary depending on your Easy-Bake Oven. 4. While the breadsticks are baking, whisk together the melted butter and garlic powder in a small bowl. 5. Once the breadsticks are done, remove them from the oven using the spatula. Brush the garlic butter mixture over the warm breadsticks and sprinkle with grated Parmesan cheese. Garnish with chopped fresh parsley if desired. 6. Enjoy your mini garlic Parmesan breadsticks while they're warm and delicious.

Chapter 4 Mug Cake Recipes

Mini Strawberry Mug Cake

Prep Time: 15 minutes | Cook Time: 12-15 minutes | Serves: 2

For the Mug Mix:
4 tablespoons all-purpose flour
2 tablespoons granulated sugar
¼ teaspoon baking powder
A pinch of salt
2 tablespoons milk
1 tablespoon unsalted butter, melted
¼ teaspoon vanilla extract
2 tablespoons diced strawberries
For the Topping:
Whipped cream.

1. Preheat your easy bake oven for 15 minutes. 2. In a small bowl, mix together the flour, granulated sugar, baking powder, and a pinch of salt. 3. In another small bowl, combine the melted unsalted butter, milk, and vanilla extract. Mix well. 4. Pour the wet ingredients into the dry ingredients and stir until you have a smooth batter. 5. Gently fold the diced strawberries into the batter. 6. Grease an oven-safe mug that fits the easy bake oven with a little butter or cooking spray. 7. Spoon the strawberry cake batter into the mug. 8. Place the mug in the baking pan and bake in the preheated oven for 12-15 minutes or until the cake has risen and is set in the center. 9. Carefully remove the mug from the oven using the spatula, as it will be hot. 10. Let the mug cake cool for 1-2 minutes. Optionally, top it with a dollop of whipped cream for a delightful strawberry shortcake experience.

Lemony Poppy Seeds Mug Cake

Prep Time: 10 minutes | Cook Time: 15 minutes | Serves: 2

4 tablespoons all-purpose flour
2 tablespoons granulated sugar
¼ teaspoon baking powder
A pinch of salt
½ teaspoon lemon zest
1 tablespoon lemon juice
2 tablespoons vegetable oil
2 tablespoons milk
¼ teaspoon vanilla extract
½ teaspoon poppy seeds

1. Preheat your easy bake oven for 15 minutes. 2. In a small bowl, mix together the flour, baking powder, granulated sugar, and a pinch of salt. 3. Add the lemon zest, lemon juice, vegetable oil, vanilla extract and milk to the dry ingredients. Mix until you have a smooth batter. 4. Gently fold in the poppy seeds into the batter. 5. Grease an oven-safe mug that fits the easy bake oven with a little butter or cooking spray. 6. Spoon the lemon poppy seed cake batter into the mug. 7. Place the mug in the baking pan and bake in the preheated oven for 12-15 minutes or until the cake has risen and is set in the center. 8. Carefully remove the mug from the oven using the spatula, as it will be hot. 9. Allow the mug cake to cool for a minute or two. Serve.

Mini Chocolate Brownie

Prep Time: 10 minutes | Cook Time: 10-15 minutes | Serves: 2

¼ cup all-purpose flour
¼ cup granulated sugar
2 tablespoons water
2 tablespoons unsweetened cocoa powder
⅛ teaspoon baking powder
A pinch of salt
1 tablespoon chocolate chips
1 tablespoon chopped nuts (optional)

1. Preheat the easy bake oven for 15 minutes. 2. In a small mixing bowl, combine the all-purpose flour, granulated sugar, unsweetened cocoa powder, baking powder, and a pinch of salt. 3. Stir in the chocolate chips and chopped nuts (if using). 4. Stir all the ingredients until well combined. 5. Grease a small oven-safe mug or use a silicone mug mold. 6. Place the brownie mix into the greased mug. 7. Add 2 tablespoons of water and stir until the mixture is smooth and well combined. 8. Place the mug in your Easy Bake Oven and bake for around 10-15 minutes. 9. Check for doneness by inserting a toothpick into the center; it should come out with a few moist crumbs. 10. Let the brownie cool for a minute before enjoying your "Mug of Joy" Brownie!

Galaxy Magic Chocolate Mug Cake

Prep Time: 10 minutes | Cook Time: 10 minutes | Serves: 2

¼ cup all-purpose flour
3 tablespoons granulated sugar
⅛ teaspoon baking powder
A pinch of salt
¼ teaspoon edible glitter or colorful sprinkles
1 tablespoon white chocolate chips
1 tablespoon blue or purple colored chocolate chips

1. Preheat the easy bake oven for 15 minutes. 2. In a small mixing bowl, combine the all-purpose flour, baking powder, granulated sugar, and a pinch of salt. 3. Add the edible glitter or colorful sprinkles, white chocolate chips, and colored chocolate chips to the dry mixture. 4. Stir all the ingredients together until well combined. Add 3 tablespoons of water and stir until the mixture is smooth and well combined. 5. Carefully transfer the mix into a microwave-safe mug. 6. Place the mug in your Easy Bake Oven and bake for around 7-10 minutes. Check for doneness by inserting a toothpick into the center; it should come out with a few moist crumbs. 7. Let the cake cool for a minute before enjoying your "Mini Galaxy Magic" Cake!

Chocolate Molten Lava Mug Cake

Prep Time: 10 minutes | Cook Time: 15 minutes | Serves: 2

¼ cup all-purpose flour
3 tablespoons granulated sugar
2 tablespoons unsweetened cocoa powder
⅛ teaspoon baking powder
A pinch of salt
1 tablespoon chocolate chips
1 tablespoon marshmallow bits (mini marshmallows)

1. Preheat the easy bake oven for 15 minutes. 2. In a small mixing bowl, combine the all-purpose flour, granulated sugar, unsweetened cocoa powder, baking powder, and a pinch of salt. 3. Add the chocolate chips and marshmallow bits to the dry mixture. 4. Stir all the ingredients together until well combined. 5. Add 3 tablespoons of water and stir until the mixture is smooth and well combined. 6. Empty the "Molten Lava Magic" Chocolate Cake Mix into the greased mug. 7. Place the mug in your Easy Bake Oven and bake for around 10-15 minutes. 8. Check for the doneness by inserting a toothpick into the center; it should come out with gooey, molten cake crumbs. 9. Allow the cake to cool for a minute before digging into your "Molten Lava Magic" Chocolate Cake!

S'mores in a Cup

Prep Time: 10 minutes | Cook Time: 10 minutes | Serves: 2

¼ cup all-purpose flour
3 tablespoons graham cracker crumbs
3 tablespoons granulated sugar
⅛ teaspoon baking powder
A pinch of salt
1 tablespoon mini chocolate chips
1 tablespoon mini marshmallows

1. Preheat the easy bake oven for 15 minutes. 2. In a small mixing bowl, combine the all-purpose flour, graham cracker crumbs, granulated sugar, baking powder, and a pinch of salt. 3. Add the mini chocolate chips and mini marshmallows to the dry mixture. 4. Stir all the ingredients together until well combined. 5. Add 3 tablespoons of water and stir until the mixture is smooth and well combined. 6. Empty the "S'mores in a Cup" Mug Mix into the greased mug. 7. Place the mug in your Easy Bake Oven and bake for around 7-10 minutes. 8. Check for doneness by inserting a toothpick into the center; it should come out with a few moist crumbs. 9. Let the "S'mores in a Cup" cool for a minute before enjoying your s'mores-inspired treat!

Colorful "Cookie Jar" Mug Cake

Prep Time: 10 minutes | Cook Time: 15 minutes | Serves: 2

¼ cup all-purpose flour
3 tablespoons granulated sugar
⅛ teaspoon baking powder
A pinch of salt
1 tablespoon rainbow sprinkles (confetti sprinkles)
1 tablespoon mini chocolate chips
½ teaspoon vanilla extract

1. Preheat the easy bake oven for 15 minutes. 2. In a small mixing bowl, combine the all-purpose flour, granulated sugar, baking powder, and a pinch of salt. 3. Add the rainbow sprinkles and mini chocolate chips to the dry mixture. 4. Add the vanilla extract to the dry ingredients and stir until well combined. Add 3 tablespoons of water and stir until the mixture is smooth and well combined. 5. Empty the "Cookie Jar Confetti" Mug Mix into the greased mug. 6. Place the mug in your Easy Bake Oven and bake for around 10-15 minutes. 7. Check for doneness by inserting a toothpick into the center; it should come out with a few moist crumbs. 8. Let the "Cookie Jar Confetti" cool for a minute before enjoying your colorful and fun mug of cookies!

Delightful Funfetti Cake

Prep Time: 10 minutes | Cook Time: 15 minutes | Serves: 2

¼ cup all-purpose flour
3 tablespoons granulated sugar
⅛ teaspoon baking powder
A pinch of salt
½ teaspoon vanilla extract
1 tablespoon rainbow sprinkles (confetti sprinkles)
2 tablespoons milk
½ tablespoon unsalted butter, melted

1. Preheat the easy bake oven for 15 minutes. 2. Combine the all-purpose flour, granulated sugar, baking powder, and a pinch of salt. 3. Add the rainbow sprinkles to the dry mixture. 4. In a separate small container, combine the milk, melted unsalted butter, and vanilla extract. 5. Pour the liquid mixture (milk, melted butter, and vanilla extract) over the dry ingredients. 6. Stir until the mixture is smooth and well combined. 7. Empty the "Mug of Dreams" Funfetti Cake Mix into the greased mug. 8. Place the mug in your Easy Bake Oven and bake for around 10-15 minutes. Check if the doneness is ready. 9. Let the "Mug of Dreams" Funfetti Cake cool for a minute before enjoying your delightful, colorful treat!

Lemon Poppy Seed Mug Cake

Prep Time: 10 minutes | Cook Time: 15 minutes | Serves: 2

¼ cup all-purpose flour
3 tablespoons granulated sugar
⅛ teaspoon baking powder
A pinch of salt
½ teaspoon lemon zest
½ teaspoon poppy seeds
½ teaspoon lemon juice
2 tablespoons milk
½ tablespoon unsalted butter, melted

1. Preheat the easy bake oven for 15 minutes. 2. In a small mixing bowl, combine the all-purpose flour, granulated sugar, baking powder, and a pinch of salt. 3. Add the lemon zest and poppy seeds to the dry mixture. 4. In a separate small container, combine the lemon juice, milk, and melted unsalted butter. Pour the liquid mixture over the dry ingredients. 5. Stir until the mixture is smooth and well combined. 6. Empty the "Mug of Sunshine" Lemon Poppy Seed Cake Mix into the greased mug. 7. Place the mug in your Easy Bake Oven and bake for around 10-15 minutes. 8. Check if it is ready or not by inserting a toothpick into the center; it should come out with a few moist crumbs. 9. Let the "Mug of Sunshine" Lemon Poppy Seed Cake cool for a minute before savoring the bright and zesty flavors!

Hot Chocolate Mug Cake

Prep Time: 10 minutes | Cook Time: 7 minutes | Serves: 4

2 tablespoons powdered hot chocolate mix
2 tablespoons all-purpose flour
1 tablespoon granulated sugar
1 tablespoon mini marshmallows
1 tablespoon mini chocolate chips
A pinch of salt
1 cup milk

1. Preheat the easy bake oven for 15 minutes. 2. In a small mixing bowl, combine the powdered hot chocolate mix, all-purpose flour, granulated sugar, mini marshmallows, mini chocolate chips, and a pinch of salt. 3. Stir all the ingredients together until well combined. Add 1 cup of milk to the mug and stir until the mixture is smooth and well combined. 4. Empty the "Cocoa Cuddles" Hot Chocolate Mug Mix into a microwave-safe mug. 5. Place the mug in your Easy Bake Oven and bake for around 5-7 minutes or until hot. 6. Carefully remove the mug from the easy bake oven (it will be hot), and stir the hot cocoa. 7. Allow it to cool for a minute before enjoying your cozy "Cocoa Cuddles" Hot Chocolate!

Matcha Mug Cake

Prep Time: 15 minutes | Cook Time: 12-15 minutes | Serves: 2

For the Mug Mix:
4 tablespoons all-purpose flour
2 tablespoons granulated sugar
¼ teaspoon baking powder
A pinch of salt
½ teaspoon matcha green tea powder
2 tablespoons milk
1 tablespoon unsalted butter, melted
¼ teaspoon vanilla extract

For the Matcha Glaze:
½ teaspoon matcha green tea powder
2 teaspoons powdered sugar
½ teaspoon milk

1. Preheat your easy bake oven for 15 minutes. 2. In a small bowl, mix together the flour, granulated sugar, baking powder, salt, and matcha green tea powder. 3. In another small bowl, combine the melted unsalted butter, milk, and vanilla extract. Mix until well combined. 4. Pour the wet ingredients into the dry ingredients and stir until you have a smooth cake batter. 5. In a separate small bowl, mix together the matcha green tea powder, powdered sugar, and milk to create the matcha glaze. Stir until smooth. 6. Grease an oven-safe mug that fits the easy bake oven with a little butter or cooking spray. 7. Spoon the cake batter into the mug. 8. Place the mug in the baking pan and bake in the preheated oven for 12-15 minutes or until the cake has risen and is set in the center. 9. Carefully remove the mug from the oven using the spatula, as it will be hot. 10. While the mug cake is still warm, drizzle the matcha glaze over the top of the cake. 11. Allow the mug cake to cool for a minute or two before enjoying your mini matcha green tea mug cake.

Cheese Blueberry Mug Cake

Prep Time: 15 minutes | Cook Time: 15 minutes | Serves: 2

For the Mug Mix:

4 tablespoons all-purpose flour

2 tablespoons granulated sugar

¼ teaspoon baking powder

A pinch of salt

2 tablespoons milk

1 tablespoon unsalted butter, melted

¼ teaspoon vanilla extract

2 tablespoons fresh or frozen blueberries

For the Cheesecake Swirl:

1 tablespoon cream cheese, softened

½ tablespoon powdered sugar

A few drops of lemon juice

1. Preheat your easy bake oven for 15 minutes. 2. In a small bowl, mix together the flour, granulated sugar, baking powder, and a pinch of salt. 3. In another small bowl, combine the melted unsalted butter, milk, and vanilla extract. Mix until well combined. 4. Pour the wet ingredients into the dry ingredients and stir until you have a smooth cake batter. 5. Gently fold in the fresh or frozen blueberries into the batter. 6. In a separate small bowl, mix together the softened cream cheese, powdered sugar, and a few drops of lemon juice (optional) until smooth. 7. Grease an oven-safe mug that fits the easy bake oven with a little butter or cooking spray. 8. Spoon half of the cake batter into the bottom of the mug. 9. Add dollops of the cheesecake mixture on top of the batter. 10. Spoon the remaining cake batter on top of the cheesecake mixture. 11. Place the mug in the baking pan and bake in the preheated oven for 12-15 minutes or until the cake has risen and is set in the center. 12. Carefully remove the mug from the oven using the spatula, as it will be hot. 13. Allow the mug cake to cool for a minute or two before enjoying your mini blueberry cheesecake mug cake.

Cinnamon Mug Cake

Prep Time: 15 minutes | Cook Time: 12-15 minutes | Serves: 2

For the Mug Mix:
4 tablespoons all-purpose flour
2 tablespoons granulated sugar
¼ teaspoon baking powder
A pinch of salt
¼ teaspoon ground cinnamon
2 tablespoons milk
1 tablespoon unsalted butter, melted
¼ teaspoon vanilla extract

Cinnamon Sugar Topping:
1 tablespoon granulated sugar
½ teaspoon ground cinnamon

1. Preheat your easy bake oven for 15 minutes. 2. In a small bowl, mix together the flour, granulated sugar, baking powder, salt, and ground cinnamon. 3. In another small bowl, combine the melted unsalted butter, milk, and vanilla extract. Mix until well combined. 4. Pour the wet ingredients into the dry ingredients and stir until you have a smooth cake batter. 5. In a separate small bowl, mix together the granulated sugar and ground cinnamon to create the cinnamon sugar topping. 6. Grease an oven-safe mug that fits the easy bake oven with a little butter or cooking spray. 7. Spoon the cake batter into the mug. 8. Place the mug in the baking pan and bake in the preheated oven for 12-15 minutes or until the cake has risen and is set in the center. 9. Carefully remove the mug from the oven using the spatula, as it will be hot. 10. While the mug cake is still warm, sprinkle the cinnamon sugar topping generously over the top of the cake. 11. Allow the mug cake to cool for a minute or two before serving.

Homemade Nutella Swirl Mug Cake

Prep Time: 10 minutes | Cook Time: 15 minutes | Serves: 2

For the Mug Mix:

4 tablespoons all-purpose flour

2 tablespoons granulated sugar

¼ teaspoon baking powder

A pinch of salt

2 tablespoons unsweetened cocoa powder

2 tablespoons milk

2 tablespoons vegetable oil

¼ teaspoon vanilla extract

For the Swirl:

1 tablespoon Nutella or hazelnut spread

1. Preheat your easy bake oven for 15 minutes. 2. In a small bowl, mix together the flour, granulated sugar, baking powder, salt, and cocoa powder. 3. Add the milk, vegetable oil, and vanilla extract to the dry ingredients. Mix until you have a smooth chocolatey batter. 4. Grease an oven-safe mug that fits the easy bake oven with a little butter or cooking spray. 5. Spoon half of the chocolate cake batter into the bottom of the mug. 6. Add a layer of Nutella on top of the batter. 7. Spoon the remaining chocolate cake batter on top of the Nutella layer. 8. Place the mug in the baking pan and bake in the preheated oven for 12-15 minutes or until the cake has risen and is set in the center. 9. Carefully remove the mug from the oven using the spatula, as it will be hot. 10. Allow the mug cake to cool for a minute or two before enjoying your mini Nutella swirl mug cake.

Chapter 5 Pies and Tarts

Fruit Vanilla Pudding Pie

Prep Time: 20 minutes | Cook Time: 10 minutes | Serves: 1

1 package pie-crust dough
1 serving vanilla pudding
Whipped cream, for decoration
Candied cherries, for decoration
Pineapple slices, for decoration

To make the crust: 1. Allow the pie-crust dough to reach room temperature, then unroll it onto a floured surface. 2. Cut a piece out of the dough, slightly larger than the Easy-Bake Oven baking pan. 3. Place the round of dough into the pan, pushing the edges up against the sides. 4. Bake for 10 minutes in the Easy-Bake Oven. 5. Remove, let it cool, and remove it from the tin. (It should come out easily.)

To make the filling: 1. Place a layer of vanilla pudding in the bottom of the cooked crust. Put the cherries and pineapple on top of the pudding. 2. Spread a generous layer of whipped cream on top of the fruit. 3. Decorate with a few more slices of pineapple and cherry.

Delicious Oreo Butterscotch Pie

Prep Time: 7 minutes | Cook Time: 10 minutes | Serves: 1

⅓ cup Oreo cookie crumbs
1 teaspoon cocoa powder
1 tablespoon sweetened condensed milk
⅛ teaspoon milk
2 tablespoons butterscotch chips, divided

1. Combine all the ingredients in a bowl except for 1 tablespoon of butterscotch chips and 1 teaspoon of cookie crumbs. Mix thoroughly. 2. Spread the mixture into the Easy-Bake Oven baking pan and bake for about 10 minutes. 3. When the baking time is over, take the pie out and allow it to cool. 4. Add the remaining cookie crumbs and butterscotch chips on top.

Sweet Lemon Pie

Prep Time:5 minutes | Cook Time: 17 minutes | Serves: 2

3 tablespoons sweetened condensed milk
1 teaspoon egg yolk
2 teaspoons lemon juice
⅛ teaspoon lemon rind, grated
1 packet sugar cookie dough
Whipped cream, for serving

1. Butter the Easy-Bake Oven baking pan. 2. Take out the sugar cookie dough and press it into the bottom of the pan and up the sides. 3. Bake in the Easy-Bake Oven for 5 minutes. 4. While it's baking, mix together the egg yolk, lemon juice, condensed milk, and grated lemon rind. 5. Remove the baked crust from the oven. Pour the lemon mixture over the crust while it's still warm. 6. Bake in the Easy-Bake Oven for 12 minutes. Allow the pie to cool completely in the pan. Spread the whipped cream on top and serve.

Easy Strawberry Pie

Prep Time:5 minutes | Cook Time: 30 minutes | Serves: 2

⅓ cup pie crust mix
4 teaspoons water
2 tablespoons strawberry pie filling

1. In a small bowl, combine the pie crust mix and water with a fork. Stir the mixture gently to form a ball. 2. Divide the dough in half, forming 2 small balls. 3. Place the dough balls on a floured board. Then roll out one ball slightly larger than the Easy-Bake Oven baking pan. Fit it into the greased pan. 4. Fill it with the pie filling. 5. Roll out the second ball of dough and place it on top. Seal the edges with a fork. 6. Bake in the Easy-Bake Oven for 25 to 30 minutes.

Coconut Lemon Pie

Prep Time:5 minutes | Cook Time: 17 minutes | Serves: 2

3 tablespoons sweetened condensed milk
1 teaspoon egg yolk
2 teaspoons lemon juice
⅛ teaspoon lemon rind, grated
1 packet sugar cookie dough
Whipped cream, for serving
2½ tablespoons desiccated coconut

1. Butter the Easy-Bake Oven baking pan. 2. Take out the sugar cookie dough. Press it into the pan and up the sides. 3. Bake in the Easy-Bake Oven for 5 minutes. 4. While it's baking, mix together the egg yolk, lemon juice, condensed milk, 2 tablespoons coconut, and grated lemon rind. 5. Remove the pan from the oven. Pour the lemon mixture onto the crust. 6. Bake in the Easy-Bake Oven for 12 minutes. Allow the pie to cool completely in the pan. 7. Spread with whipped cream and serve.

Flavorful Cherry Pie

Prep Time:5 minutes | Cook Time: 30 minutes | Serves: 2

⅓ cup pie crust mix
4 teaspoons water
6 teaspoon cherry pie filling

1. In a small bowl, combine the pie crust mix and water with a fork. Stir the mixture gently to form a ball. 2. Divide the dough in half, forming 2 small balls. 3. On a floured board, roll out one ball slightly larger than the Easy-Bake Oven baking pan. Fit it into the greased pan. 4. Fill with the pie filling. 5. Roll out the second ball of dough and place it on top. Seal the edges with a fork. 6. Bake in the Easy-Bake Oven for 25 to 30 minutes.

Yummy Blueberry Pie

Prep Time:5 minutes | Cook Time: 30 minutes | Serves: 2

⅓ cup pie crust mix
4 teaspoons water
6 teaspoons blueberry
pie filling

1. In a small bowl, combine the pie crust mix and water with a fork. Stir the mixture gently to form a ball. 2. Divide the dough in half, forming 2 small balls. 3. On a floured board, roll out one ball slightly larger than the Easy-Bake Oven baking pan. Fit it into the greased pan. 4. Fill with the pie filling. 5. Roll out the second ball of dough and place it on top. Seal the edges with a fork. 6. Bake in the Easy-Bake Oven for 25 to 30 minutes.

Classic Apple Pie

Prep Time:5 minutes | Cook Time: 30 minutes | Serves: 2

⅓ cup pie crust mix
4 teaspoons water
6 teaspoon apple pie
filling

1. In a small bowl, combine the pie crust mix and water with a fork. Stir the mixture gently to form a ball. 2. Divide the dough in half, forming 2 small balls. 3. On a floured board, roll out one ball slightly larger than the Easy-Bake Oven baking pan. Fit it into the greased pan. 4. Fill with the pie filling. 5. Roll out the second ball of dough and place it on top. Seal the edges with a fork. 6. Bake in the Easy-Bake Oven for 25 to 30 minutes.

Berries Tart

Prep Time:5 minutes | Cook Time: 5-8 minutes | Serves: 2

7 teaspoons shortening
7 teaspoons sugar
Pinch of salt
¼ cup flour
⅛ teaspoon baking powder
⅛ teaspoon vanilla extract
For the Topping:
4 strawberries, sliced
6 blueberries
Whipped cream
Individual size container vanilla pudding

1. Cream together the shortening, sugar, and salt in a bowl. 2. Add the flour, baking powder, and vanilla. Mix until a ball of dough forms. 3. Sprinkle 1 teaspoon of flour on the countertop. Roll the tart dough out, then use a knife to cut it into 1-inch circles. 4. Place the tarts on a greased Easy-Bake Oven baking pan. You may need to cook in batches. 5. Bake for 5 minutes in the Easy-Bake Oven. Wait for the tarts to cool, then remove them from the oven. 6. Spread some vanilla pudding on top of each tart, add some fruit, and top with whipped cream.

Delicious Caramel Apple Tart

Prep Time:5 minutes | Cook Time: 12 minutes | Serves: 2

1 packet sugar cookie dough
3 teaspoons sweetened condensed milk
1 teaspoon egg yolk
2 teaspoons apple juice
1 teaspoon caramel topping
¼ apple, cut into small slices, for serving
Whipped cream, for serving

1. Take out the cookie dough and press it into a greased Easy-Bake Oven baking pan and up its sides. 2. Bake in the Easy-Bake Oven for 5 minutes. 3. Meanwhile, mix the egg yolk, apple juice, and condensed milk in a bowl. 4. Pour the mixture onto the crust. 5. Bake in the Easy-Bake Oven for 12 minutes. 6. Cool the completely in the pan. 7. Run a knife around the edge of the tart, then turn it over gently. Do NOT touch the apple center. 8. Apply the caramel topping and whipped cream around the outside of the tart and garnish it with apple slices on top.

Traditional Apple Pie

Prep Time: 10 minutes | Cook Time: 25 minutes | Serves: 3

⅓ cup pie crust mix
4 teaspoons water
6 teaspoons pie filling;
apple

1. Plug in your Easy-Bake Ultimate Oven and preheat for 15 minutes. 2. Mix the pie crust and water in a small bowl with a fork until a ball forms. 3. Cut the dough in half and roll each half into a small ball. Roll out one ball on a board dusted with flour until it's bigger than the baking pan. 4. Place in an oiled baking pan. 5. Put pie filling inside. 6. Roll out the other piece of dough and put it on top. Use a fork to seal the edges. 7. Lay the baking pan into the Easy-Bake Ultimate Oven's baking slot. 8. With the help of a pan pusher, push the baking pan into the baking chamber. 9. Adjust the cooking time to 25 minutes and bake. 10. After the cooking time ends, push the baking pan into the cooling chamber with the help of a pan pusher. 11. Allow it to cool for 5 minutes. 12. When cooling is done, with the help of a spatula, remove the baking pan from the oven. 13. Serve and enjoy.

Vanilla Blueberry Danish

Prep Time: 10 minutes | Cook Time: 20 minutes | Serves: 4

¼ cup biscuit mix
¾ teaspoon sugar
½ tablespoon margarine
4 teaspoons milk
½ tablespoon blueberry
pie filling
To Make Frosting:
¼ cup powdered sugar
1 teaspoon water
2 drops vanilla

1. Plug in your Easy-Bake Ultimate Oven and preheat for 15 minutes. 2. Mix cookie mix, sugar, and margarine. Mix until it looks like crumbs. 3. Add the milk and stir well until you have a soft dough. 4. Drop ½ teaspoon onto a baking pan that has been lightly oiled. Press indentation in the center with your thumb. Fill the indentation with blueberry pie filling. 5. Lay the baking pan into the Easy-Bake Ultimate Oven's baking slot. 6. With the help of a pan pusher, push the baking pan into the baking chamber. 7. Adjust the cooking time to 20 minutes and bake. 8. After the cooking time ends, push the baking pan into the cooling chamber with the help of a pan pusher. Allow it to cool for 5 minutes. 9. When cooling is done, with the help of a spatula, remove the baking pan from the oven. 10. Pour frosting over the top of the Danish with the help of a spatula. 11. Serve and Enjoy.

Chapter 6 Mixes and Frostings

Colored Sugar Mix

Prep Time: 5 minutes | Cook Time: 0 minutes | Serves: 4

2 tablespoons sugar
2 to 3 drops food coloring (for vibrant colors) or 1 drop food coloring (for softer colors)

1. Put sugar in a plastic bag that is big enough for a snack. Choose your favorite food coloring and then close it up tightly. 2. Cover the sugar carefully with your fingers, then shake the mixture until it turns the color you want. 3. Use more sugar or a very small drop of coloring for every 2 tablespoons of sugar to make a very light pink color. 4. Use the plastic bag to store extra.

Basic Yellow Cake Mix

Prep Time: 5 minutes | Cook Time: 0 minutes | Serves: 6

6 teaspoons flour
4 teaspoons sugar
¼ teaspoon baking powder
Dash salt
2 teaspoons shortening

1. Mix all the ingredients together well. 2. Put in a ziplock bag and close it up until you need it.

Simple Butter Bisquick Mix

Prep Time: 5 minutes | Cook Time: 0 minutes | Serves: 12

8 cups of flour
4 tablespoons sugar
4 tablespoons baking powder
4 teaspoons salt
1 cup butter

1. In a big bowl, mix the flour, baking powder, salt, and sugar together well. 2. With a pastry blender, cut in the butter until the mixture looks like fine breadcrumbs. 3. Keep in a sealed jar until you need it.

Classic Chocolate Cake Mix

Prep Time: 5 minutes | Cook Time: 0 minutes | Serves: 11

1 cup sugar
3 tablespoons unsweetened cocoa powder
1½ cups all-purpose flour
1 teaspoon baking soda
½ teaspoon salt
⅓ cup butter

1. Add the cocoa powder, flour, sugar, baking soda, and salt to a medium-sized bowl. 2. To mix, use a wire whisk to mix it all together. 3. You can use a pastry blender to blend in the butter until the mixture looks like fine crumbs. 4. Put about a ⅓ cup of the mixture into each of the 11 small cans with caps that fit tightly or zip lock bags. 5. Keep it somewhere cool and dry.

Butter Oats Cookie Mix

Prep Time: 5 minutes | Cook Time: 0 minutes | Serves: 8

1½ cups quick cook oats
¾ cup all-purpose flour
¼ cup baking soda
¾ cup brown sugar, packed
½ cup butter

1. Add the oats, flour, baking soda, and brown sugar to a medium-sized bowl. Mix by stirring. If you use a pastry cutter, cut in the butter until the mixture looks like fine breadcrumbs. 2. Put about half a cup of the mixture into each of 8 small containers or zip lock bags that have lids that fit closed. 3. Close the lids and write the date and what's inside on the labels. Keep it somewhere cool and dry. Within 12 weeks, use.

Buttercream Frosting

Prep Time: 5 minutes | Cook Time: 0 minutes | Serves: 6

2 cups powdered sugar; sifted
3 tablespoons instant non-fat milk powder
6 tablespoons butter

1. Mix powdered milk and sugar together. Use a pastry blender to cut in the butter. Put about a third of a cup of the mixture into each of eight small containers or Ziploc bags. 2. Close up tight. Label with the date and what's inside. 3. Keep in a cool, dry place. Keep it for 12 weeks.

Cream Cheese Frosting

Prep Time: 5 minutes | Cook Time: 0 minutes | Serves: 8

1 cup powdered sugar, sifted
4½ teaspoons instant nonfat milk powder
3 tablespoons cream cheese

1. Use a wire whisk to mix the powdered sugar and milk powder together. You can use a pastry cutter or a fork to mix in the cream cheese. 2. There should be about a third of a cup of the mixture in each of the 8 small containers or zip lock bags. 3. Close the lids and write the date and what's inside on the labels. Keep it somewhere cool and dry.

Colored Sparkling Frosting

Prep Time: 5 minutes | Cook Time: 0 minutes | Serves: 6

4 teaspoons vegetable shortening or butter
⅔ cup powdered sugar
¼ teaspoon vanilla
2 teaspoons milk
Colored sugar crystals for decoration

1. Shortening, powdered sugar, vanilla, and milk should all be mixed together in a small bowl until the mixture is smooth and fluffy. 2. Put two teaspoons of frosting on top of the first layer. 3. Add the second layer and keep topping it. Add colored sparkling sugars on top.

Chocolate Butter Frosting Mix

Prep Time: 5 minutes | Cook Time: 0 minutes | Serves: 9

2 cups powdered sugar, sifted
3 tablespoons nonfat dry milk powder
½ cup unsweetened cocoa powder
6 tablespoons butter

1. Put the cocoa powder, milk powder, and powdered sugar in a medium-sized bowl. (If thick, sift.) 2. Cut the butter into the dough with a pastry cutter until it looks like fine breadcrumbs. 3. There should be about a third of a cup of the mixture in each of the 9 small containers or zip lock bags. 4. Close the lids and write the date and what's inside on the labels. Keep it somewhere cool and dry.

Conclusion

In drawing the final curtain on "The Easy Bake Oven Recipe Book," we're not just closing a cookbook but inviting you to start a lifelong culinary experience. This collection of recipes is more than just a compendium of baking instructions; it's a testament to the enduring magic of the Easy Bake Oven. It's a tribute to the generations of young chefs who have donned aprons, mixed ingredients, and eagerly peered into that tiny, glowing chamber of creation. It's a celebration of the simple joys that come from crafting miniature masterpieces with your own hands.

As you close this book may the lessons you've learned and the recipes you've mastered continue to inspire you. May you keep experimenting, exploring, and sharing your delicious creations with the world. May the warm glow of the Easy Bake Oven forever remind you that the magic of baking is not confined to the kitchen but resides in the hearts of those who bake with passion and love.

Appendix 1 Measurement Conversion Chart

WEIGHT EQUIVALENTS

US STANDARD	METRIC (APPROXINATE)
1 ounce	28 g
2 ounces	57 g
5 ounces	142 g
10 ounces	284 g
15 ounces	425 g
16 ounces (1 pound)	455 g
1.5pounds	680 g
2pounds	907 g

VOLUME EQUIVALENTS (DRY)

US STANDARD	METRIC (APPROXIMATE)
⅛ teaspoon	0.5 mL
¼ teaspoon	1 mL
½ teaspoon	2 mL
¾ teaspoon	4 mL
1 teaspoon	5 mL
1 tablespoon	15 mL
¼ cup	59 mL
½ cup	118 mL
¾ cup	177 mL
1 cup	235 mL
2 cups	475 mL
3 cups	700 mL
4 cups	1 L

TEMPERATURES EQUIVALENTS

FAHRENHEIT(F)	CELSIUS (C) (APPROXIMATE)
225 °F	107 °C
250 °F	120 °C
275 °F	135 °C
300 °F	150 °C
325 °F	160 °C
350 °F	180 °C
375 °F	190 °C
400 °F	205 °C
425 °F	220 °C
450 °F	235 °C
475 °F	245 °C
500 °F	260 °C

VOLUME EQUIVALENTS (LIQUID)

US STANDARD	US STANDARD (OUNCES)	METRIC (APPROXIMATE)
2 tablespoons	1 fl.oz	30 mL
¼ cup	2 fl.oz	60 mL
½ cup	4 fl.oz	120 mL
1 cup	8 fl.oz	240 mL
1½ cup	12 fl.oz	355 mL
2 cups or 1 pint	16 fl.oz	475 mL
4 cups or 1 quart	32 fl.oz	1 L
1 gallon	128 fl.oz	4 L

Appendix 2 Recipes Index

Made in the USA
Columbia, SC
03 December 2024

48330883R00062